About the Author

Ken Mellor was born and brought up in Leeds. His father and grandfather were already established in the local cinema trade, so it was no surprise that his early years were steeped in cinema lore.

An electrical apprenticeship was interrupted by a three-year engagement in the Royal Air Force. It was during this period of military service that his interest in location film work was rekindled by the arrival on camp of a film unit.

At an early age he inherited from his father an interest in vintage motorcycles and has over the years taken part in many nationwide events.

Before joining the film industry, he also spent some years in Speedway racing, a sport he had followed from early teen years. Moderate success resulted in being appointed captain of the Aldershot team in 1960.

He now lives near Selby in North Yorkshire and continues to lead an active life by running a specialist record company and continuing his passion for vintage motorcycles.

JUST A SOUND GUY

Ken Mellor

JUST A SOUND GUY

The Life of a Film and Television Sound Recordist

Vanguard Press

VANGUARD PAPERBACK

© Copyright 2014
Ken Mellor

A CIP catalogue record for this title is
available from the British Library.

ISBN 978 1 84386 786 9

*Vanguard Press is an imprint of
Pegasus Elliot Mackenzie Publishers Ltd.*
www.pegasuspublishers.com

First published 2014

**Vanguard Press
Sheraton House Castle Park
Cambridge England**

Printed & bound in Great Britain

INTRODUCTION

Several times during the preparation of the book, I was asked if there was going to be a dedication and to whom. As the accompanying photograph will convey, it is my dear old Dad who receives the honour with the following citation. For passing to me all the mechanical skills, interests across such a wide range of subjects, patience and dedication to the task in hand and above all else, a sense of humour based on his long held theory, that if they laugh with you, they won't laugh at you. If amongst all these traits there happens to be a microscopic amount of modesty, then I safely qualify to call myself a 'Chip off the old block'.

In recalling many stories from the past, there are the inevitable pauses to reflect on faces that were once an everyday part of my working life but are no longer with us. Many of them live on in the following pages each achieving his or her 'fifteen minutes of fame', which is a timely way of saying that for all of us, the present is slipping into the past with every tick of the clock; whilst the future remains, as always, the great enigma. Only the past is real.

Those that need an acknowledgement are already listed in the book and I thank them for being a part of that past. I am never sure of the correct time in human life when we enjoy or deplore a retrospective survey, so to anyone who was there with me may I apologise for hiding their identity under a literal cloak of anonymity.

Many of the photographs were taken by me or with my camera, however, as always I have acquired a collection of photographs from many sources, and to my regret I did not record that ownership. May I, therefore, offer my apologies for those that appear with no credit. Finally, I have to thank David Gyimah for suggesting the original idea and while the end result has not produced any great oaks from little acorns, I hope the reader will feel that at least the ugly duckling of an idea has turned into a magnificent swan of a story that is worth enduring beyond the opening pages.

CHAPTER ONE

OVERTURE AND BEGINNERS

The swinging sixties were three years old as I made my way into the myriad of streets just a whistleblow from Marylebone Station. It was an area that could evoke such wonderful poetic observations that I imagined John Betjemin may have described it thus, "Along Rodmarton Street blackened houses stand humbly displaying their blistered paint. No touch of Voysey here. No leaning to the styles of Nash or Blore. Just leaning." I was looking for the Screen School where I was hoping to enrol for one of the evening courses on Film Sound technique. There were day courses, but at a much higher fee and most of the places seem to have been taken by applicants from overseas. But two nights each week over a period of four months was within my budget. Just. As I entered one of the blackened buildings, there was an immediate impression of past times. Wooden stairways showed years of wear. Paint was peeling from everywhere that paint had been applied and each door with a glass panel seemed to have a crack that ran across the corner, invariably on the right-hand side and almost always at a regulation distance of six inches from the corner.

Two rooms had been allotted for the use of tuition. In addition to the principles of location sound, another course dealt with the camera department which would soon lead into a situation of 'them and us'. I was never quite sure how Screen School operated on a firm business footing. A larger room was used for dance instruction and rehearsal, also for shooting an occasional television commercial. Rumour had it that at weekends events of a more unsavoury nature took place, but as I was never in this part of London on a Saturday night I was never able to confirm this. Before any instruction began students were offered a manual compiled by the school. This was a comprehensive listing of all sound and camera equipment, along with specifications and diagrammatic illustrations. It was well put together and gave the whole organisation an air of professionalism. It was also unwise to refuse the asking price of £7 if you wanted to ingratiate yourself with the instructor. This also applied to the hi-fi speaker cabinets he built in his spare time. As he took your cash he would smile meekly and say, "Well it helps to oil the wheels." Was this a salutary lesson in life I wondered.

The appendage of the word 'school' was something of a misnomer as there were no rows of regimented desks, nor any hint of strictness. On this first evening there were nineteen students, including a girl, who sat down to begin what we all hoped would bring changes to our lives. Yes there would be written theory, mainly on a Tuesday evening. But Thursday evenings would, where possible, be given over to visits to recording studios (there were two within walking distance) and to dubbing, editing and transfer suites.

There were 'hands on' sessions with film recording equipment of a doubtful age, although it was unlikely that any of us would ever come across it if and when we graduated.

Although the theory could be tedious, taking in the science of sound waves, along with the working of the human ear and the principles of how we perceive sound, it was pure enthusiasm which carried us along, even when the instructor came out with such throw away remarks as. "When you have carried 40lbs of equipment up three flights of stairs to a location, you'll wonder why you spent four months learning about the theory of sound." One of his other morale boosting phrases ran along the lines of, "I want the information on my notes to appear in your notes without it entering either of our minds." I never did quite grasp his subtle logic but I presumed that he meant to say, "You need more than stars in your eyes to survive in film or television."

The first of a number of guest speakers came on the second Thursday and as I was an avid reader of screen credits, the name was familiar to me. This was Sound Recordist, Ernie Cousins who had a number of feature films under his belt. He was the archetypal Londoner. A ready wit and raconteur without much prompting and able to convey his knowledge in simple words. Furthermore, he had brought along some 'state of the art' microphones and the Rolls Royce of the film recording world, the Series 3 Nagra tape recorder. A model that was only introduced around 1961 and here were we, able to touch it, turn the controls and even lace up the recording tape. It was like Manna from Heaven. Little did I realise that Ernie was soon to become a mentor who's teaching ranged from how to be an unpaid sound apprentice to learning Cockney rhyming slang! Even more uncanny was that some twenty years into the future when I was on the regional committee of the film technicians trade union, then known as. The Association of Cinematograph Television & Allied Technicians (ACTT), Ernie and I would meet up at the Annual Conference.

*

The visit of Ernie had made an impact on the class. His breezy presence bringing a charge of eagerness to us all. A sort of antidote to the acerbic style in which our instructor delivered his epigrams. Little did we know that the next guest two weeks later would come in like a March wind, making an impression that one did not easily forget. This was Ken Cameron of Anvil Recording Studios, a company he had formed in 1952 with other colleagues who found themselves redundant with the closing of the Crown Film Unit. This organisation had been an arm of the Government, linked to the Ministry of Information and responsible for a steady output of films during world war two planned to maintain the nation's mettle. As Sound Engineer for the unit, Ken had been responsible for recording much of the stirring music which was to lift many hearts in cinemas across war torn Britain. In later years, in collaboration with the conductor, Muir Mathieson, he recorded much of the music for British Transport Films. In amongst all this, he managed to write two books on film sound which became standard reference works in the industry for years to come. As recognition of his services to the film industry, he was awarded the OBE in 1950, all at the age of 35. As an aside, I should mention that he was the younger brother of James Cameron, that intrepid BBC reporter who brought us stories from all over the world during the sixties and seventies and was still working in 1984 at the age of 73.

So this was the man who came to the Screen School to implant his knowledge upon us. He claimed to be an ardent Scot, hence the kilt he was wearing and frequently did, but facts prove otherwise. Although born of Scottish parents, it was in the County of Buckinghamshire where he first drew breath, moving to Scotland while still a schoolboy. Nevertheless, he made a striking figure as he launched into a story about his Scottish ancestry. He claimed his Great Grandfather had been killed at the Battle of the Little Bighorn. Well not actually in the battle. He had been camping in the next field and went over to complain about the noise! It was a brilliant opener and he had our attention from then on. As a bonus we were invited to make an evening trip to the Anvil Studios at Beaconsfield. Now all that remained was to work out how many cars were needed to transport nineteen students.

Before that visit took place there was more theory to be taken in. Two representatives from equipment manufacturers came along to demonstrate the latest range of microphones and tape recorders designed for professional use.

I suspect that the companies did this on a no fee basis, using the opportunity for publicity purposes to promote their products. I don't suppose it did the Screen School accounts any harm either! One evening was given over to combining the sound and camera courses to enable students in both classes to realise the difficulties that might arise when a cameraman has established a scene, only to find the soundman would like to place his microphone somewhere in the shot. In later years I too was to find it could lead to some friction when you appeared with what some cameramen called the 'shadow machine'. However, I was always aided by some advice given to me by Ernie Cousins when I once asked him how he dealt with the problem. He merely said, "Tell them where you are going to put it but do it with dignity." I never did know whether he was being satirical or just did not want to offend my provincial ears.

The evening trip to Beaconsfield Studios was planned to leave from central London at six p.m. It was a tight call for some which meant only fourteen students could make it, easing the car transport problem. We arrived at the studios just in time for the first rehearsal of the film score for a Hammer horror film entitled The Evil of Frankenstein. It provided a fascinating insight into how much time and effort is spent providing the background music which is so vital to taking the audience on a roller coaster ride of emotion. In charge of the session was Ken Cameron, who, despite trying to keep control of musicians, technicians and at the same time obtain a near perfect sound balance, found time to welcome us and show some of the finer points in what he was trying to achieve. He also ensured we were included in the refreshment break an hour or so later. Scottish hospitality at its finest! It was back to basics the following week. We were now past the halfway stage in our course and as if to illustrate that the world of film sound recording was not all glamour, our instructor brought us down to earth with two nights of plugs and connectors. Like so many things in life, there is no 'one size fits all' despite repeated attempts at worldwide standardisation. If the situation was chaotic in 1963 then fifty years on into the Twenty-first Century has seen very little advance. Nevertheless, it was essential that we knew which wire went where, all the more so when it came to wiring up the now standard 3-pin 13 amp plug.

Although first introduced in 1947 it was less than twenty years ago that I came across the old 2-pin 15 amp plug on church premises while setting up an organ recording session. Input connections along with microphone plugs could also be confusing as some manufacturers adopted their own system. So although it could be mind numbing to have to try and absorb all this information, I like to think of the occasions when the instructor was right when he said, "One day you will thank me for it." With the analytical calm of hindsight, I often looked back on his delivery of knowledge and how it appeared in our notes, remembering his quote about, "Not wanting it to enter our minds." But his manner was plausible which made you want to listen. He also possessed a flair for remembering names, which he would use when addressing the class and was a very effective way of making someone who considered themselves not very important, of suddenly being in the spotlight of attention. I have to confess that I too tried to adapt this memory of just a name as a means of communicating when making a first contact, even to a point of recommending it to anyone who was taking the first steps in the freelance world.

An oft quoted expression is, "It's not what you know but who you know." It could be implied that there is a hint of nepotism in the meaning nevertheless, to be able to recall the name of someone you met or were working with several months earlier, can be a very productive way of opening doors.

For one visit we had to split into two groups spread over the same number of weeks, due to the confines of the film dubbing suite. This was where the sounds recorded on location were transferred to 16mm or 35mm magnetic tape, which could be run alongside the actual film. It was also our introduction to optical film where a magazine of normal 35mm film ran through a camera without a lens, the sound being recorded optically onto the film. Those who stayed behind at the Screen School were entertained to a superb collection of 'out takes', pre dating by several years that popular TV programme 'It'll Be Alright on the Night'.

As the year drew to a close, the world was stunned by the assassination of President Kennedy. The aftermath in central London brought onto the streets what is commonplace now, but ground breaking at the time. The television news crew and 'vox pops' with reporters seeking the opinions of all and sundry. American style television reporting was here to stay. It had of course been a big year for major news stories. The Great Train Robbers had netted a million pounds. Martin Luther King had his Dream, while the Tory Government was rocked by the Profumo scandal .The thought that in years ahead I was to feature in many headline news stories never entered my head. As Shakespeare said, "Some men are born great, some achieve greatness, while others have it thrust upon them." Which one was I?

By now the class was becoming almost a social occasion. Everyone was on first name terms and much of the knowledge we had gained was often the source for fierce debate. If it was going to be put to the test in the years ahead the signs were that it may be a struggle. Business confidence was low, as was morale in the Tory party. Alec Douglas Hume, who had replaced Harold Macmillan, was struggling to gain the support of his ministers. Pundits were already looking ahead to a General Election and signs were that both major parties were becoming more and more aware of the power that television could play to impart their policies upon the electorate. Whether or not this registered with any of the students at Screen School is just speculation, but there was the realisation that, as television became more mobile with a growing number of programmes made away from studios, the need for staff and the job opportunities was growing. And this of course was why we had all enrolled for the course in the first place. But now perhaps what was uppermost in our minds, was what would happen on the last night... One thing the course had achieved was a full complement of students throughout the twelve week period, which must have said something about the style of our instructor's tuition, despite his somewhat downbeat outlook on life.

Where he had acquired his grounding for passing on these gems of human behaviourism was never made clear. He did have a definite knowledge of sound theory and electronics, but his academic qualifications were unknown. There were certainly gaps in some of his understanding of history, for example, when Ken Cameron came to visit the class and told the story of how his Great Grandfather had been killed at the Battle of Little Bighorn, I had a sneaking impression that our instructor confused the location with that of Rorke's Drift. Not only the wrong war, but a different continent! Just which one of us came up with the suggestion of a small presentation for him, I have now forgotten. But as he was a pipe smoker it seemed appropriate to find something that would give added pleasure. When we made the bestowal he was genuinely overcome, but managed to say, "You are all wonderful" And so we came to the final night of our course.

As I walked down from Marylebone Road, everything looked the same. Up ahead of me I could see two other students on the other side of the road, while two others were coming in the opposite direction. The only difference was, in front of the entrance to Screen School were two taxi cabs, both discharging fares. I recognised the instructors but not the other pair. No one expected any great celebration on the final night. No lining up in front of the Principal awaiting your name to be called. No grand ceremony of throwing mortar boards in the air and certainly no tables drooping under the weight of canapes and savoury dishes. The only noticeable difference was, we were all to gather in the room where the camera course had been held, it being larger.

One of the unrecognised faces was the Principal, although I may be using a word not chosen by him. The other stranger was Shaw Taylor, who was already making a name for himself on television with his Police Five crime busting series. I don't suppose he imagined he would still be presenting the programme in 1992! Even less imaginable was that fifteen years hence, I would be his recordist on a number of episodes. Perhaps I should at this point draw your attention to a story about Dorothy Parker, the American short story writer and wit. She is reputed to have passed little notes to certain guests who were leaving one of her sumptuous dinner parties, wishing them a safe journey home and adding, "Here is a list of all the names you have dropped during the evening." I must, therefore, crave your indulgence for the names I shall drop! Inevitably, in this industry, loosely called show business, for those who work out of sight behind the camera, they are often in close proximity to the action around them... No matter how passionate or violent the scene may appear, at close hand are any number of technicians. So as I recall the passing years, these names and people are integral pieces in the story.

Shaw's reason for being there was to pass out the Certificates we had earned. These were not a guaranteed CV into the film or television world, but they did state the subjects covered and 'hands on' experience gained, plus they looked good to any prospective employer. A list of over fifty film and television companies was included with the suggestion that you bombard them with job seeking letters. Shaw only stayed a short time, which may have had a bearing on the fee he was being paid!

Nevertheless, he was able to pass on some home spun advice about this industry we were all hoping to launch into. His first was, "If it sounds too good to be true, it probably is." Another was, and I think he borrowed this from Sam Goldwyn, "A verbal contract isn't worth the paper it's written on." All delivered in a delightfully flippant style. It was a happy occasion, and I doubt if there was not one amongst us who thought, *This is the life for me*. I could, though, not help recalling one of the many philosophical phrases that our instructor had delivered over the past twelve weeks, which was, "If you are hoping to earn a living in the film world, expect to see more lunchtimes than lunches."

Shaw's parting shot before leaving was intended to add a little morale to our group. I think? He left us with the following advice to guide us through the topsy-turvy world of film and television. First he reminded us that the world did not owe us a living and that the only way to gain experience, was to live life!

At the time I doubt if any one of us had such deep thoughts. We were about to start out on our crusade armed with a Certificate! It could only be the adrenalin of youth that was driving us on. We piled out of the Screen School for the last time and, apart from three or four who had to rely on public transport, headed for one of the late night coffee bars in Baker Street. Here, above the clatter and Cappuccino, pledges were made, allegiances formed. A standard letter of application was drafted with several variations to send off to employment officers on our list. One student volunteered to print a newsletter that could be used to share ideas and list any vacancies and other relevant information. The world really was our oyster.

CHAPTER TWO

CURTAIN UP!

This was going to be the real world. I kept remembering another of our instructor's satirical comments when he said, "If you are going to stick your head above the battlements and say, here I am, then you have to avoid the brickbats that may come your way." The idea of sending off a string of letters did not appeal to me, knowing there may be eighteen others to be considered before mine. My plan was to try and obtain a job, any job, that would give me a first step on the ladder. My first interview was with a Mr Jake Levy, who ran a record company by the name of Oriole from a third floor office somewhere off Oxford Street. It seems his only claim to fame had been a 78rpm record entitled 'Freight Train' that had reached number nine in the charts in May, 1957. Inside what passed for his office was a desk and one chair. His! Leaving me to stand awkwardly without leaning. He handed me a single sheet of music and asked did I know the right way up. My answer in the affirmative must have impressed him for he immediately replied, "I can offer you six pounds a week." That would barely cover my rent and food bill, without considering the running costs of a 1954 Morris Minor. "Think about it, give it some time," he said as he opened the door. I did! All the time it took me to go down three flights of stairs.

My next application had possibilities. A direct connection with the film business. This was a film editing facility in west London. Upon enquiring what the job entailed, I was informed that it mainly consisted of ferrying edited films across London on a bicycle! Several more non starters made me realise, it was time to play my 'ace in the hole'. During the visit of Ernie Cousins to Screen School I had been bold enough to ask if there may be any opportunities to join him sometime on location, just to look over his shoulder. Adding that I lived in south west London, not too far from Merton Park Studios, one of the small independents that still survived in London.

At this time my budget did not run to a telephone, so it meant ringing from a call box or writing. People who have to work away from home are not likely to have time to reply to trivia. I did have another ploy, which was casually dropping in on someone on the pretext of being in the area, but as I was already using this as a means of obtaining an occasional meal, I did not want to gain a reputation as a scrounger. I combined the two. I rang Ernie saying I was in the area and could I call. He said yes and suggested staying for a meal. The perfect combination!

Being freelance, Ernie had several strings to his bow. In addition to his location work, he serviced equipment for companies and individuals and was shortly to be engaged on installing new film recording equipment at Merton Park Studios. Furthermore, I was welcome to come along and help on an unpaid basis. He told me that the Recording Manager was Fred Turtle and to be sure I asked for him. The reason for the precaution was, Fred had acquired the 'nickname' Harry Kipper and, not unnaturally, did not look kindly on anyone who used it. The girls who worked in the front office, charming as I am sure they were, did have a mischievous sense of humour and it was not unknown for them to direct someone who asked for the sound department along the corridor with the instruction to, "Ask for Harry Kipper." Forewarned is to be forearmed, and I arrived on the day and met Fred, who turned out to be a most delightful person.

It was not just a case of looking over Ernie's shoulder. I was another pair of hands to help lift in the film recorders, or thread endless cables into conduit, ensuring they were correctly labelled before doing so. And on an odd occasion, I even got to make the tea! It was during this experience that I sampled Cockney humour first hand. I had long thought that, despite an almost savage streak to it, in there somewhere was a glint of humanity but there always remained a slight barrier. A sort of 'us and them'. All the time I worked with Ernie I was usually known as, 'mate', 'cock', 'mush', or 'sprog'. On the second day while taking a breather from lifting, Ernie displayed true Cockney humour and humanity. A young man of Asian origin came in and handed a piece of paper to him and remained as if waiting for a reply. Ernie began reading the memo aloud: "To the Sound Department. With effect from today, will all short ends of magnetic tape be retained for possible further use for voice over work." Ernie took a pencil from behind his ear as if to use it to drive home his reply, and said, "Who's bright idea is this? Where are you from?"

The young man puffed out his chest and proudly declared, "Ceylon."

Ernie, already frustrated from the day's work, almost exploded into a reply with, "Cor Blimey! I didn't think you were from bleeding Wapping. I meant what department?" Then came the humanity. Seeing the confusion on his face, Ernie put a hand on his shoulder and said, "Don't worry son, I'll sort it out." The young man left somewhat bewildered, trying to work out the connection to his homeland and Wapping.

At the end of three days I had an elated feeling. Having been at the sharp end of a film studio dubbing suite and mingling with technicians who worked in studios and out on location, I was convincing myself that it was only a matter of time before someone would be in touch with an offer I wouldn't refuse. Ernie had nothing in his diary for the immediate future, but as we parted he called out to, "Keep in touch." At least that was a comforting thought.

Three more job vacancies were applied for. I was using a little bit more of the instructor's philosophy, who suggested that interviews were good experience and even if you did not have the qualifications they were looking for, some organisations paid expenses. I only found one that did, and even then they were only talking tube fares. Summer came and went along with a large portion of my bank account, saved only by supplementary work. I telephoned Ernie who suggested I go along and meet him at a film equipment exhibition that was being held at Westminster Hall.

He was sharing a stand with a manufacturer of sound recording accessories so it would be an ideal place to meet likeminded fellows. And so it proved, while helping Ernie on the stand I could look reasonably intelligent and steer any questions to the right person It was here that Ernie introduced me to a name I was already very familiar with. Peter Handford. Peter had a long list of feature film credits, such as Room at the Top, The Entertainer, Saturday Night and Sunday Morning and Billy Liar. We also shared a passion for recording the sounds of the steam locomotive, which were slowly disappearing from the railways of Britain. Peter had started in the mid fifties and now had secured a contract with a specialist record company. For my part, I had been issuing tape recordings, packaged for enthusiasts but sales were not providing a living income.

Perhaps the turning point in my career happened when Ernie asked me if I would like to join them for a meal, adding that it was his treat for my help during the day. For the next two hours I sat enthralled listening to their recollections. Both had started in the industry before the outbreak of world war two and despite the problems and working conditions they endured, they nevertheless, returned to location film sound at the end of hostilities. Before leaving, Peter passed on details of a producer who had an office near Waterloo Station. He specialised in short films for the cinema and also had distribution overseas to some of the old Commonwealth countries. Television had taken away much of his work opportunities and productions were now on very low budgets. So much so that he had apparently crossed swords with the film union on more than one occasion over rates of pay. At this stage in my career I didn't seem to have much to lose and as Peter suggested that I use his name as a means of introduction, I made an appointment to meet him.

A film producer with an office in London has a kind of grandiose ring about it, but as the last few months had taught me in my trudging round seeking employment, London seemed to be brimming with these little empires up flights of narrow stairs, usually with low powered lighting and no doubt, rents to match. However, that old saying of 'never judge the contents by the picture on the box' came true, for despite the district and the entrance to the building, inside his office was an air of almost opulence. Big desk, bright lighting, comfortable chairs and a choice of tea or coffee! He outlined the background to his company's work, stressing that there would be no lavish locations or luxurious hotels. Meals may be meagre and irregular and that rates of pay may not be what I was used to.

That I had not yet been accustomed to rates of pay went some way to giving him my answer when he finally said, "Well, what do you think?" His next production was a series of eight minute films designed as programme 'fillers' for cinemas in Britain and overseas. The subjects were to show life in Britain with themes as diverse as industry, farming, sport, leisure and social history. There were to be possibly twelve films in the series with the first due to start in two months. The remainder were scheduled for 1965. With nothing more than a handshake, I left his office on the understanding that I would in due course be contacted with details of the first location.

When the package arrived it contained a wealth of details from equipment required to a provisional shooting script, along with the location. This was a forge and rolling mill at Scunthorpe Steel Works. His warning of no lavish locations was no threat! I met up with the rest of the crew on location, just a cameraman and an assistant, along with the director who came from Greece and had brought a limited knowledge of English with him! We were booked for two days shooting in this very unglamorous huge building, where sparks seemed to fly in every direction and men were constantly wiping the perspiration from their faces, all to a background of the glow from the furnaces. The noise was unbelievable from a recordist point, but as there was no dialogue in the shooting schedule, it looked like being an easy initiation or perhaps baptism of fire may have been more appropriate, in view of the heat from the furnaces.

The second day was made up of finding out how these 'men of steel' relaxed at the end of a punishing day enduring the heat and excruciating noise, to say nothing of the constant danger from molten metal pouring from spouts, huge billets of almost white hot steel passing along rollers and cranes moving overhead. All of this was long before the Government Legislation concerning health and safety in the workplace. With everything 'in the can', Lenny, the Greek director tried to make me feel welcome, for he delivered, in his best English, some words of encouragement along the lines of, "Me, you work more. Good job." I had the feeling he was being complimentary!

Vin, the cameraman, was more direct. "Fancy doing any other shoots? If so give me a card." It was in his hand before he could continue. But it was to be a long wait until the next job. As I drove back to London, there may have been a smile of satisfaction on my face, but my stomach was telling me that the old instructor wasn't far wrong when he warned about seeing more lunchtimes than lunches. It was to be a constant worry for a few more years to come.

It was several months before I received details of another location assignment. Again it was in the north of England and in my home county of Yorkshire. This time the subject was, 'The Englishman and his Leisure time' with this particular episode covering greyhound racing, showing the extremes of the sport in Britain, from the huge stadiums down to what were colloquially known as, 'Flapping Tracks'. The first one was Doncaster, probably chosen because their facility fee was much lower than others who were approached by researchers. I had by now become acutely aware of just how low the budgets were for this company. Once again the cameraman was Vin. But we had a new director. Barry was one of the new school. Dark hair, dashing looks and sporting one of the fashionable suede overcoats. On the race night he could have easily mingled with the punters. We were also joined by a second sound recordist, Les Brumpton. Little was I to know then that this was the start of a long friendship , sharing not only a preoccupation in sound recording but a penchant for cinema organs and fairground organs.

We began the shoot with the usual arrivals and track activity, then as the racing got under way, we covered crowd scenes, bookies, kennel maids, owners and the dogs. Barry felt he had enough material and, having already made friends with several owners, we retired to the stadium clubhouse to enjoy some local hospitality. As we stood and chatted, the subject came round to where were we filming next and Barry informed the group. It was clear there was shock. One nice middle aged lady put her hand to her mouth and said, "Oh dear."

Another slightly rotund gentleman with a glowing face, took a deep breath, then exhaled and said, "Rather you than me lad. I should keep your hand on your wallet."

We were then bombarded with advice about what to and not to do. Barry, perhaps in his innocence, came up with, "Oh we'll be all right, Ken comes from around here!" I didn't know whether to feel proud or ashamed.

We arrived at the 'flapping' track stadium in the late afternoon. I use the word stadium somewhat loosely, as it was situated alongside a spoil heap from the nearby coal mine. On one side was a car scrap yard, on the other side were the railway sidings loaded with coal trucks awaiting collection. Already there was activity, which seemed to mainly comprise owners exercising their dogs. Who would then bend and examine closely any deposit left by the dog. Over on the far side, smoke was already coming from a shed, upon which was written in white paint, REFRESHMENT'S. The use of the apostrophe trying hard to give some culture to the setting. Who ever had been responsible, tried even harder, for below was painted the word, TEA'S.

We were looking to meet a man named Harry, who we had been told would be wearing a flat cap, but he found us with a greeting along the lines of, "Ayeup, ata lads fromt films, dussa wanta sup o tee?" I had sensed Barry was uneasy from the moment we had arrived. The south Yorkshire dialect has a harshness that can be delivered at a machine gun pace. I was brought up in Leeds with it's much flatter vowel sounds, bordering almost on the Dales localism, but even I could be confused. As an example, I served three years in the Royal Air Force with a colleague from Sheffield, and even towards the end of our service, there were some words that were not immediately clear. Barry seemed to be coping by using a simple formula of recognising the last word of each sentence, to understand what Harry was saying!

Within minutes a young girl was approaching with a tray of mugs which contained a strong brew of 'apostrophe tea'. Knowing we had come up from London, someone had thoughtfully added a bowl of cube sugar! We had to go through the motions by showing how grateful we were. When Les returned from parking the camera car, I pointed to a mug and said, "That one is yours."

Les delivered one of his classic wisecracks by saying, "No thanks I haven't got time to chew it!" We were following a plan that Barry had devised for security. Parking the vehicle where we could see it. Carrying the minimum of equipment and as little money as possible, well out of sight and only obtainable by a body search.

As little money as possible prompted Vin to say, "On what you are paying us, that won't be difficult." Barry was out of earshot at the time!

Barry said to Vin, "What I want to show is the roughness."

"That won't be a problem," said Vin. "It's all rough."

"And yet it has a quaintness that is typically English," added Barry.

"Yes, it's dog rough," said Vin.

So that was to be the theme. Contrast the dogs, the equipment, the people. Yes the people. You could have devoted the whole film to them. Especially the one who latched onto Barry. Without being too indelicate, you would have to describe her as big! "Eeh are ute fella from London? Tha can cum home wi me anytime. Al let thee put coil on mi fire any neet ot week." Poor Barry, he didn't deserve it and worse still, he didn't know how to cope with it.

Les didn't help matters by adding such comments as, "Play your cards right and you're in there, Barry."

So we filmed the rough. Just like Vin said, it wasn't difficult. An old Ford car engine drove the hare, which, in reality was a bunch of old rags. The dogs were running on a mixture of sand and coal dust, and catering was down to a couple of housewives who brought in a few loaves, sausages and beans. We just packed up the equipment and went. We looked for Harry but couldn't make him out. Everyone was dressed in a flat cap.

There is an old saying in the film and entertainment business which says, 'never work with animals.' This was certainly the case on the next film, which was to feature zoos and circuses. If you have seen one zoo, you have seen them all was the general feeling, but the producer had the notion that large reptiles would make an audience squeamish, especially crocodiles. So off we went to where they had a large reptile house. Barry by now was maturing as a director and was looking for new angles all the time. The zoo staff had separated this particular crocodile into a pool where we had complete access without any interference from the public. That didn't make it any easier to film and nobody was keen in venturing too close to obtain the type of shots Barry was looking for. Nor did we take any comfort from the keeper who said, "It's still digesting the last meal so it should be fairly docile."

Vin, ever the statistician, asked where did 'fairly' come in a scale of one to ten, to which the keeper replied with a straight face, "Somewhere between one and ten."

Les had not been available for this shoot, so Vin had brought along his sister, who had a hankering to join the film business, to take over as a boom swinger.

From a sound point, there was little in the way of 'atmos' (short for atmosphere or general ambience in a room or building). So I suggested just putting a gun microphone on the end of a boom pole and extending it across the pool to capture any splashing, there already being the sound of running water. When I looked across at Carol, she was holding the microphone about a metre above the crocodile and I was just about to say, "Hold it a little higher," but I never finished the sentence. The crocodile had launched itself up and bitten around ten centimetres from the end of the capsule.

"That's docile is it?" said Vin.

All I could think about was what I would tell the company who had hired me the microphone when I returned it to their stores. "Sorry Guv, a crocodile did it!"

On the plus side, we did have film evidence of the whole sequence as Vin had turned over before the 'action' call. On the return to London, it had been planned that we call at a riding school that trained circus horses. "You can't go wrong with horses," Barry assured Vin. "Always make nice pictures." The school had a complete circus ring complete with seats, dummy people, banners and music, which did have potential to 'make nice pictures'. After seeing some of the horses training around the ring, each one with a girl rider, Barry had one of his notions. "Ground shots are OK, but what I would like is a motion shot from the saddle."

"On yer bike," said Vin (or something similar)!

"I didn't mean you. Give the mute camera to one of the girls," Barry almost snapped back. "Have the five horses going round with a girl and the camera on the last one."

Vin could see the sense in that and started loading the camera. Meanwhile Barry had suggested the head girl to be the one on the last horse and started instructing her as to the type of shot he was looking for above the ears and to complete three circuits before pressing the button on a signal from him. It all started well and by the end of the second circuit, Barry was feeling pleased with himself. The girl was in a low position, the horses were behaving perfectly it had all the hallmarks of a classic shot. Then he gave her the signal and she pressed the camera button right on cue. It must have taken all of two seconds for the horse to hear the clatter, whine and shutter rattle of an unblimped

35mm film camera just above its ears. The effect was almost horrific. First it reared, throwing the girl, still clutching the camera, over the rump. Then it bolted towards the exit colliding with a wooden screen before falling and trapping itself under some horse jump barriers. A trapped horse is not something to be near when legs and hooves are thrashing, but luckily there were enough knowledgeable girls on hand to quieten the animal and return it to all fours, whereupon, the first thing it did was to unashamedly relieve itself.

As for the girl with the camera. She had fallen into the sawdust ring and was surprisingly unhurt. Even more remarkable, the camera battery lead was still attached and the camera was still turning. Vin, in his stoic way, picked it up, removed the film and said, "I'll have to mark this film as NBG!"

Was this the end of the matter? We never found out. I know Barry, who had been physically disturbed by the incident, went and had some words with the owner of the riding school. On the surface, the horse seemed to have survived the fall, but whether any claim was made against the production company, we never knew. One thing it did not deter Barry from wanting, was a shot he failed to obtain at the greyhound tracks we had attended. He had this notion to try and film a greyhound in huge close-up as it waited to see the hare go flying by.

He imagined he could capture the pent up emotion, eagerness and hunger to race, all in the dog's eyes and expression. So once again we found ourselves at a small greyhound stadium on a non race day. "I only want five seconds," Barry kept telling Vin, and the dog owner, and the kennel maid, who patiently kept putting the dog into the trap. Each time it came forward, then retreated when it saw this person with a weird looking box, making a whirring sound that may have reminded it of something that happened the last time it attended the vets.

"Maybe if we had the hare going by it would help." This was another of Barry's ideas. Showing great fortitude, the owner started up the hare mechanism. As it neared the traps, the dog could hear the familiar sound and made ready to leap out, until, that is, Vin put in his appearance.

By now patience was being stretched very thin. Not only amongst the crew but the staff and the dog's owner. Again the director in Barry rose to the surface. "Would it be possible to startle it by bursting a balloon?" I think the moment he said it he realised it was a foolish thing to say.

So too did the owner, muttering something like, "This is damn ridiculous." He snatched the dog, attached its lead and strode off towards his car. And that was the end of Barry's bright idea. All except for Vin who thought he would make a contribution.

"A pistol might have had the right effect. But that's the same as bursting a balloon," said Barry.

Vin began walking towards the camera car, but called out, "No, I meant between the eyes."

I don't think there was any particular order for making the series of films. Some of the stories were still being researched almost up to arriving on location. This was certainly the case with the film about one of England's stately homes. The setting was Hagley Hall, in Worcestershire, the home of Lord and Lady Cobham. Lord Cobham had in fact been the last Governor General of New Zealand. Lenny the Greek was to be the director and I was pleased to read on the call sheet that Les was back on the sound crew. This proved even more fortuitous when we found the farm house where we booked in, was just down the road from a wonderful collection of fairground organs. The purpose of choosing Hagley Hall was to do with a story about two members of the Gunpowder Plot, who were caught sheltering there in January, 1606. Their presence was given away by the cook and another servant, who became suspicious at the amount of food that was being eaten, plus they had glimpsed two strangers in an upstairs room. Lenny could see no real significance in the Gunpowder Plot story as his knowledge of English history, if his knowledge of the language was anything to go by, must have been zero. But he could appreciate the fine architecture and views across the park.

We met at the Hall and were shown into a reception room. Both Les and I were fearful of how Lenny would cope with the language when addressing Lord Cobham.

Though he lacked basic small talk, he had picked up a string of, what the BBC used to call 'oaths', somewhere along the way. Possibly in the kitchens of Greek restaurants, as he boasted regularly that his brother owned three of them in north London. Help was at hand though, for on this shoot, the producer had seen fit to employ a Production Assistant by the name of Margaret. At least she should be able to convey Lenny's wishes to His Grace.

The problem was, that Lenny, now he had seen inside the Hall, began to have ideas about featuring servants depicting those who had been the informants all those years ago. He knew in his mind what he wanted to film, but conveying it in words of a few syllables was not easy. By now, Lord Cobham was beginning to suspect that the original agreed facility fee to film the exterior of the Hall and grounds, was being taken a little too liberally to include the interior, and should have been arranged prior to our arrival and not, as he put it, "Over the doorstep."

Margaret managed to be the 'go between' in deciding what and where we could film and we started to walk towards the entrance hall, when Lord Cobham called, "If it's of any help to you, I have a friend who has a helicopter who might be willing to give you some aerial views. Do you want me to give him a ring?"

Lenny knew the meaning of the word helicopter, and said, "Yes please Lord, ring."

We waited outside. Lenny was already at work planning and drawing the angles of approach to get the best shots. "Must fly right high up, very important to have right high. I was tempted to make some light hearted comment about planning the Dambusters Raid, but decided against, knowing it would fall on stony ground where Lenny was concerned.

A half hour or so later, Lord Cobham's butler came down with a message. "The pilot was willing to provide the helicopter for half an hour but all preparation and fuel costs must be met."

Gleefully, Lenny said, "Yes, Yes, you bill, we pay."

The butler looked at Lenny, squared his shoulders and with a delivery that has been imitated a thousand times from Erich von Stroheim to Kenneth More, said, "Very good, Sir."

As the light was good, Vin decided on a few general views of the Hall and park and finished off with some close ups to end the roll. If the weather held, the aerial views should be stunning. Lenny phrased it as, "Tomorrow we make one damn good movie." We stowed the gear and headed off to the farmhouse bed and breakfast. The helicopter was booked for eleven a.m. and we made sure everyone was there and prepared in good time. Sure enough, around eleven, the sound of an approaching helicopter was heard and minutes later it appeared over the Hall and landed in an adjacent paddock. It was immediately clear that there was only one seat next to the pilot for Vin. No place for Lenny to do his directing from, which did not please him and he went into a string of, presumably, Greek profanities. With time ticking away, Vin climbed aboard and they lifted off.

As the helicopter came in for the first pass over the Hall, Lenny began ranting with such broken phrases as, "Too much high, go under," or perhaps, "Under low, get up." All of which was accompanied by words known only to him, the most popular one seemed to be, "Ay, Ay Shustkos."

With the helicopter back on the ground and Vin satisfied in what he had obtained, one might have thought that was the end of the matter. But Lenny was not happy.

So much so that he said he was going away to rest. "My head is over my heels. Everybody here tomorrow, nine o'clock – rest of day off!" Les and I did not hesitate. We were off to spend a most enjoyable time at the museum of fairground organs, where we were made welcome by the owner, Bill Barlow. It even resulted in going back at a later date to record the entire collection.

Back at the farmhouse, although not included in the tariff, we were invited to join the owner and his wife for an evening meal. They had some people coming who were also members of the local drama group, and it was to be a dress rehearsal of their period costumes. Lenny was also there and upon seeing the dresses, suddenly said, "We got cook and servant for film." It was a brilliant thought and totally out of character for Lenny, but brilliant, nevertheless.

Fortunately, Margaret was on hand to expand the idea to the group and explain just what would be involved. The matter of the period of the dress could be overlooked, for in the words of many a journalist: "Why lose a good story for the sake of a few facts!"

Lenny now had the 'bit between his teeth'. His next suggestion caused near panic amongst the amateur actors, when he told them he wanted to film them next morning and with two of them delivering some lines. Normally the group did one production a year, and spent eleven months rehearsing. Les threw in the suggestion that we could use 'idiot boards' for the dialogue. He was, however, tactful enough to use the word 'prompt'. So we selected two of them to take the part of the cook and servant. Two others also suggested they were available, being retired. Suddenly Lenny had a crowd scene! Margaret devised some simple dialogue which included such period words as, Thou, Verily and Thee and soon had a script ready.

The difficult part was how to film it close to the Hall, without arousing any attention. Lenny had command of the situation. It was as if he had received some divine intervention the way he laid out the scene. A simple two shot, established, then walking through frame and delivering the lines. "Then it's in the box." He may have meant 'bag', but no one was going to correct him at this late hour. We already knew a little of the routine at the Hall and thought around lunchtime to be the best time. Staff would be occupied on other duties and Lord Cobham may even take a nap after his lunch.

We arrived next morning as planned. The staff had become accustomed to seeing us filming in the park, so nothing out of the ordinary there. We had rehearsed the whole scene back at the farmhouse a dozen times so it should work. We set up the camera, brought in the two background 'extras', then the two principles who walked through perfectly, delivered the lines as rehearsed and disappeared out of frame. Les was happy with the movement. I said, "OK for sound." Vin called for an end board and the shot was in the 'box'! Lenny just looked smug.

That was the last time I saw Lenny. I did hear that he had left the film business, but I always had him down as a survivor. I fancy he dined out a few times on the story of how he saved the film by duping an 'English Lord'. Probably in a Greek restaurant!

For the next film, the crew, mainly Vin and myself, received our 'comeuppance' at the hands of a club comedian who was later to rise to television stardom. This was Larry Grayson, although at the time, he was just another 'turn' at a working men's club in Coventry. It was to be another look at leisure time in England, although what they made of it in Tanganyika or Northern Rhodesia I cannot imagine.

We were only looking for a few moments but Larry, true professional as he was, even at that stage of his career, turned us into part of his act, using us in his patter. It went something like, "You see the one with the camera, that's Tarquin. He's anyone's for a doughnut. He can only see with one eye. You don't know if he's looking at you or trying to see the clock. I said to him what a big lens you've got, I'll bet you can see your way in the dark." The audience, mainly car workers from the Rootes factories, loved it.

Then it was my turn.

"The one with the headphones, that's Quentin. He's a lovely man. He collects knitting patterns. He looks after the sound, he listens to what's going on. I wouldn't like him in the room next to me! I said to him this morning, I bet your ears could tell a few stories doing your job. Do you know what he said? Pardon."

It went on for another ten minutes. Even after we had run out of film! We were just as helpless as the audience. Fifteen years later, when Larry's career was riding high, I worked with him on a charity show. I told him I was now living in a village near Nuneaton, his home town, and he replied, "Do you know, I always wanted to open a wool shop there."

A look at farming in Britain seemed a nice picturesque subject to round off 1966. What I didn't know at this stage, was that there were changes ahead for both Les and I. But all that was in the future. The producer wanted a typical farm for this story. Not one of the new sprawling multi acre set ups that were now spreading across Cambridgeshire and Norfolk. He may also have been thinking about the size of the facility fee too. Derbyshire seemed to be the ideal location. Hills, stone walls, a mixture of sheep and cattle. It all seemed quintessentially English.

We arrived in pouring rain. No one had thought about wellington boots. It was a sea of mud and slurry from the moment we got out of the vehicle. I was never a 'snappy dresser', but I did have a preference for suede shoes. What a mistake it was on this day. Barry was the director and he thought it may improve. 'Townies' always did try and sound knowledgeable about country life. He was wrong this time, however. It was still raining hard by the time the cows were brought in for milking. Barry thought there might be something worth filming, aided perhaps by the farmer's two daughters, who took an active part in running the farm, including milking. Vin suggested that Barry should try his hand to which one of the girls agreed. "Just sit here," said the daughter. "I'll take your hands and show you where to put them." The cow enjoyed it and the girl wasn't complaining, but it was too much for him.

"No, I think we'll just settle for a long shot," said the clearly embarrassed Barry. It was an early start the next day to see the cows trooping out of the milking parlour into the fields. Barry felt it was the shot that would make the film worthwhile, especially as the sun was just appearing above the hill, creating low shadows so beloved by cameramen and directors. As the cattle moved across the field, they were in both light and shade, prompting Vin to be at his creative best.

The whole film became a delight to work on. There were no stoppages for retakes. No tantrums. No incidents. Not even a hair in the gate! Maybe because the sun had shone all day. As Les summed up, "What a difference a day makes."

As Christmas neared, Les rang me about the new franchises that had been awarded. Yorkshire was to have its own television region, which, not surprisingly was to be known as Yorkshire Television. They were to start building a library of programmes on film ready for the opening date in September, 1968. This meant there would be a great deal of work in the north during this period and after when the station was up and running. His final remark was, "How about moving up north and working together?" It was a tempting thought. I still had this equation over lunches and lunchtimes! I decided to do it.

CHAPTER THREE

THE SECOND ACT: "NEW HORIZONS"

The first thing to do was to establish a plan of campaign. It seemed that there were already other technicians moving into the region looking for the prospect of work so we would not be alone. But how to sell ourselves? Les came up with, "Why don't we just go around and make ourselves known. We scrub up well, we have the equipment; it's only a matter of shaking the hand of unit managers." So, nothing ventured, nothing gained, we set about touring as many Heads of Film departments as we were able to make contact with, leaving a business card each time. It took time, but slowly the phone began to ring more. First with Tyne Tees, who had the franchise for that area. Then Yorkshire Television, Granada, Border Television and the new franchise holders for the London area, Thames Television and London Weekend. The last named were to provide a great deal of work through their programme, World of Sport, which became a rival of the long established BBC Grandstand. They too were to use Les and I and it was always a tricky situation to try and keep a balance between the two, avoiding any mention that you had been working for the rival.

When I look at my work diaries for this period, it is staggering to see the distances covered in one day. One example shows an early start to Teeside to record interviews with Evonne

Goolagong, a rising tennis star and a Wimbledon winner in 1971. Also Jaroslav Drobny, who had been a tennis star in the fifties. Then it was over to Liverpool to record Eric Sawyer, the Chairman of Liverpool FC. Then down to Nottingham to try and interview Tony Hateley, who had just hit the headlines as the first footballing millionaire. This was ironic for only a few weeks earlier, I had again been at Middlesbrough, this time with Wilf Mannion who was one of the first footballers to earn a £10 weekly wage. Wilf was of course one of the members of the England team, when all five of the forwards had a name beginning with the letter 'M'. Award yourself one point for each one of the other four you can name. The work load over the next three years steadily grew. Both Les and myself had made more contacts with other recordists, with the result that it became common to pass work on at such time when you had bookings for the same dates and did not want to let your client down. If you were double booked, I suppose it would be human nature to pick the best job. But that was not always the way it worked out. Jim McKee, from Glasgow and one of the old school of recordists, passed a job on to me which sounded like sailing out to a North Sea oil rig just to do some general shots and a piece to camera. However, it turned out to be the launch and location of a new design of rig in the BP Forties Field, being named 'Highland One'. To take all the dignitaries and press out, BP had hired a Danish mini cruiser from DFDS, the 'Skipper Clements'. This sailed out of Leith and for the next four days, we were wined and dined courtesy of BP. There was even one occasion when caviar was served!

Our work plan had started off by each one of us establishing ten contacts. The idea being that if each one provided ten days work in a year, then that would be a basic existence. Anything above that would be a bonus. But like the best laid plans, there were snags. Political unrest and uncertainty about a change of Government did not do much to boost confidence. The problems in Northern Ireland were growing, although it was providing work. Les had been over twice working for Ulster Television. There was a pleasant interlude in the summer. Peter Handford rang to say he was coming to Yorkshire on location for the feature film, The Railway Children, and could we perhaps meet. When I mentioned that things were quiet workwise, he then suggested that I join him for two days as his maintenance staff, for which he would pay a fee. This generous offer was typical of Peter and a guide to his personality.

He had a wonderful sense of humour at many levels. He had a great affection for the old music hall double acts. To such an extent he would sometimes arrange patter with a colleague along the lines of, "Your face is very familiar, where have I seen you before?" To which the other would reply: "Oh! I'm out of there now."

He also had his word game for pompous types. When I was living in London, we met several times at audio exhibitions. I recall one young sales executive who was using big words to Peter, probably having marked him down as some old hi-fi buff from nowhersville, commenting on some piece of equipment as an anachronism. Peter looked at him and said, "That means spiders doesn't it?"

"No you are thinking of arachnids," said the young man in a haughty tone.

"No they're in Egypt," said Peter, and walked away leaving a very deflated ego.

When he was feeling mischievous, he would stretch a rubber band across an effects microphone and wait for the moment the clapperboard closed, then twang the band. Dubbing suite editors always knew who the sound mixer was on one of Peter's films.

Being based in the north of England did not mean that all film work originated there. Assignment Officers in London could have a fairly limited knowledge of Britain. Much of which often appeared to have been culled from little more than a map of England in a pocket diary. Two classic stories from the offices of BBC and ITN, and I leave it to you to ponder which one to allot one or the other to, may help to illustrate this. During the crisis in Northern Ireland, both sides agreed to peace talks at Leeds Castle. A brief came down to the assignment desk to send a crew with a start time of nine a.m. Three rooms were booked at the Dragonara Hotel, in Leeds, being confirmed with a Telex message. Next morning around nine a.m. an anxious reporter was on the phone asking for the name of the hotel where his crew were booked in, adding he had just arrived at Maidstone Station and was about to take a taxi to the venue. To find his crew were 240 miles away in Yorkshire when Leeds Castle was just five miles from Maidstone in Kent was not what he wanted to hear.

Another assignment called for a crew to be sent to Northampton to cover an industrial dispute and overnight accommodation was to be booked. Not being immediately aware of the location of Northampton and not finding a hotel listed in the standard listings register, he put trained logic into motion. He knew North Shields was across the river from South Shields, so it must follow that the same applied here. He also noted that as there was a hotel listed for Southampton, he booked the crew in there.

Unbelievable? In later pages there is a story about us filming in Middlesbrough and receiving an urgent call to get to Stavanger, Norway, because we were the nearest crew! There was a light hearted notion that assignment officers and film operations managers, imagined that once you drove past Rickmansworth and Aylesbury, the land became wild, hilly and industrial. All except Norfolk, which was very flat, because Noel Coward had said so!

So it was no surprise to be booked for a London based programme about the selection and training of Justices of the Peace in Walsall and driving more miles than a London crew would have done. The same applied to a story about brick making in Peterborough, which was to be another of those miniscule documentaries that would appear through the Round window, or maybe the Oval window of Playschool.

While all this may indicate an idyllic and carefree way to earn a living, there were dangers which, before the age of Health and Safety Regulations, were either pushed into the background or simply never considered An example happened while on location for a film about 'ERNIE'. (No not Morecambe and Wise, they appear later). This was a film for the UK Government National Savings, to be used to promote the sales of Premium Bonds and also to entertain audiences at the visitor centre at Lytham in Lancashire.

The script was based on a 'spoof' James Bond theme, where an international criminal mastermind plots to break into the site, rig the machine known as ERNIE to indicate his numbers and clean out the Government coffers. Most of it was shot at night with such traditional scenes as a dinghy landing on a deserted beach, frogmen discarding their gear and running across sand dunes and of course there had to be a black Mercedes with a tall female Chinese chauffeur dressed in black. When it came to her big scene, the director asked if she had driven an automatic car before. She replied no. Which was not unusual – thousands of drivers have not. He assured her that it was all automatic, just requiring the lever moving to 'D' and pressing the right hand pedal. Simple! The girl was obviously using a well known actor's ploy by always saying yes when you are asked, "Can you...?" What she failed to say was that she had never driven a car before!

It was a simple enough shot, calling for her to drive up to the iron gates, the villain would get out, slip a card into the electronic lock and the gates would open.

The approaching car would start from 50 metres away and was to be filmed from behind the gates with camera and sound crew side by side.

She was sitting in the car with the engine running, possibly thinking, *if it starts automatically, it must stop automatically*. When 'action' was called, she moved the lever and pressed the pedal. The car was probably approaching 35 miles an hour when it hit the gates. Luckily, the ground bolts had been withdrawn, which saved the occupants from serious injury. When the car was perhaps 10 metres from the gate, I knew instinctively it couldn't possibly stop. Something made me grab hold of my colleague, Ken Ashton, by the collar and we both jumped clear. The table with the Nagra recorder was not so lucky.

The left hand gate hit the camera tripod, scattering Paul, the cameraman and his assistant, who had realised very late that the car was not going to stop. Both received injuries. Paul, especially so. The camera viewfinder having been pushed into his eye socket. The Mercedes had embedded itself into the rear of a parked vehicle. Stunned onlookers finally arrived to rescue the actors from the car, while Ken and I looked after the camera crew. Paul was lying with his leg in a strange position, but fortunately it was not broken. However, his eye was already looking very swollen. That was the end of filming for the night and all we could do was recover the equipment. To our amazement, the Nagra recorder was still turning. It continued to do so for the rest of the week. One reason why they are built like a tank and cost an arm and two legs! The crew were shaken and definitely stirred!

We still had another week of filming and Sunday had been scheduled as a rest day. However, in view of the injuries, the production company also pencilled in Saturday for most of the crew. But it would mean an early start on Monday. The new week started with a string of interviews with celebrities who were going to enthuse about Premium Bonds, with a recommendation that you go out and buy some.

The odyssey began in Yorkshire with Harvey Smith and Geoff Boycott, then Ian Botham and Leslie Crowther in Nottingham. Across to Birmingham to visit ex footballer Billy Wright and his wife, who was one of the Beverley Sisters. Noelle Gordon of Crossroads fame was on our list, but had to cancel due to a virus. This meant a shorter working day for which we were grateful.

Tuesday found us heading for London with more interviews lined up. These were Diana Dors, Raymond Baxter, Reginald Bosanquet of ITN 'News at Ten' and Henry Cooper. Wednesday was almost a rest day. It was spent at the production offices completing all the paper work and log sheets for film and tape. Also for drawing more stock for the remaining scenes.

Richard, the director was worried that, despite all the 'A' names being nice about Bonds, he didn't have an ordinary member of the public saying they had won any money. He did not want to stage it in London or some other urban centre. His vision was to find some old rustic out in the 'sticks', who had won. So after much studying of maps, we left the next day and headed west to take in some remote areas of Wiltshire, Gloucestershire, Herefordshire and Monmouthshire.

We kept away from main routes and picked out villages with delightful pastoral names, such as Ogbourn St. George, Duntisbourn Abbots, Much Marcle and Mitcheltroy Common. All to no avail. We asked fifty people in farmyards, blacksmiths, village stores, country inns, a travelling library, a filling station with only one pump, road menders, a ladies keep fit class and a troop of bell ringers. Not one amongst them had ever been a Premium Bond winner. Richard was beginning to flag. His faith in the percentage of winners told to him in the very room where ERNIE sat whirring away was becoming meaningless.

"One more day then we drop the whole idea." were the last words I heard him say, as he bade us goodnight with a slam of his bedroom door. As we were leaving the hotel, the local postman arrived on his GPO bicycle. His answer was in the negative. So too was that of the level crossing keeper just down the road. And so it went on, at least another twenty times. By now the director's gloom had spread to the whole crew. Nobody was saying, 'Try him', or 'Let's give her a try', or 'Why not knock on that door?' The couldn't-care-less attitude was spreading.

We were driving into a wide valley. It was typical mid Wales country. Gentle sloping fields, low rounded hills, irregular hedges. In one of the fields was a man with two dogs moving a flock of fifty or more sheep towards some small enclosures. "Let's go through the motions," said Richard. It must have been a strange sight for the shepherd. Five people heading his way carrying film equipment. The dogs froze. Even the sheep stopped milling around. We were already rolling as we approached. "Morning," said Richard. "We're making a film about Premium Bonds, just wondered if you've ever bought any and won anything?"

"Won a hundred pounds four months ago," was the reply. It was mesmerising. I looked at the camera to make sure it was turning. The Nagra was recording, Ken had the gun mic. Right alongside Richard. We had got it! Richard's next question was something like, "What did it do for you?" He was told how it was used to decorate the house, improve the kitchen and build a patio. All delivered in a lovely lilting South Wales accent.

As we all walked back down the field, Richard borrowed a line from Edith Nesbit's book, 'The Railway Children'. "It will be ice buns for tea tonight children". We drove to Monmouth, booked in at the Beaufort Arms Hotel and held an end of picture party.

The seventies was a troublesome decade when compared to the carefree swinging sixties. The problems in Northern Ireland were reaching proportions never seen before on the streets of Britain. Strikes plagued major industries and spilled over into domestic life as postal workers, civil servants and public service workers raised the total of more working days lost since the 1926 General Strike. The big news stories were coming from Northern Ireland. Les had already been over several times working for Ulster Television and as we both carried each other's business card, he had passed one of mine to an NBC reporter in Belfast.

The American Network had offices over here, along with reporters, using mainly British technicians for stories covering Britain and Europe. So began my introduction to war torn Belfast, which did not get off to a good start. One of the first stories was at night in an army outpost down the Falls Road and, like any diligent recordist would do to obtain a level, I switched on a small pocket torch. No sooner had I done so I was struck by a sandbag, hurled by an infuriated sergeant with the curt instruction to douse the light. The military liaison officer quickly explained to me about the danger of snipers sited in the high rise blocks of flats. Needless to say, I didn't need to be told a second time!

Life in Belfast, while tinged with excitement, could be stressful with a constant need to be aware of who you spoke to, a parked vehicle or package, vague instructions to be at a certain point to cover a breaking story and never display any indication of a National flag. To come back to the mainland and work on a simple story such as Playschool or Nationwide was pure recuperation. Or as some of us called it, "The pit pony syndrome." They too spent all their working days in the dark, except for when the pit closed for the annual holiday and they were brought to the surface and put in a field, spending the first hour running around kicking their legs in the air. How do I know all this? I had already worked on a programme about pit ponies for, yes, you've guessed it. Playschool!

Edward Heath was installed at Number 10 in June, 1970. This did nothing to dispel the political unrest. Wildcat strikes and disputes were becoming known as the 'English Disease', resulting in more foreign crews covering stories on the mainland, in addition to the already heavy coverage in Northern Ireland. German television stations seemed obsessed with what was happening and their crews were sometimes to be seen filming in front of the army lines. We just hoped they were being paid enough 'danger money'. As 1970 drew to a close, it would have been easy to become depressed with the work load. Gone were many of the films made for overseas which always looked at the gentle side of English Life. Now there was a hungry need for 'hard' news. Not only to service the daily bulletins, but in-depth programmes with titles such as, '24 Hours', 'Midweek', 'Panorama', 'Newsnight', and 'World in Action'. The next three years were going to broaden my horizons, literally! However, on the plus side, it was pleasing to note that, by and large, the lunches were keeping pace with the lunchtimes!

It had been some months since Les and I had actually worked together, although we kept in regular contact. He had just finished a particularly hard stint in Belfast, so it came as no surprise when he told me he was linking up with a cameraman who had a contract to service the news bulletins for BBC North. The area covered would mean he stayed in Yorkshire and as he put it, become a jobbing sound recordist. It was regular Monday to Friday work and he seemed happy with the idea.

As for me I just waited for the phone to ring, which fortunately, it did more and more. It was a real round robin of jobs for both BBC and ITV, covering such programmes as, Tomorrow's World, That's Life, On the Ball, Ask Aspel, Record Breakers and This is Your Life, or TIYL. The code word it was known by to prevent any possible leaks. Even the clapperboard had to be marked with only a production number. There was still a steady output of films from the Central Office of Information, or COI, the Government Department that looked after entertaining the former Commonwealth countries. Only now their gamut had taken in Latin American counties. This often brought a second reporter on location to record a commentary in the appropriate language.

In earlier pages I mentioned about my horizons being broadened. It was now about to happen. I was covering a story about the collapse of Rolls Royce, when I received an urgent call from NBC to go to Belfast. The first British troops had been shot and the situation was expected to escalate. It did tend to be a policy of NBC to overact to situations and go in with 'all guns blazing' to a point of saturation coverage. But that was probably what made them a first class news channel. I arrived in Belfast and booked in at the Europa Hotel. This had become the centre for all press and media crews. I checked with the NBC duty reporter, expecting to be allotted to a cameraman for the following day, but was immediately asked if my passport and overseas inoculations were up to date. I was able to inform him they were. "Something big is happening on the other side of the world, how do you feel about it?"

When you are tired from a long journey and had been looking forward to a comfortable bed, words do not always immediately register. The other side of where? I had started to think he was meaning the other side of the city. And why would he want to know how I felt about it. Americans do have a way of expressing themselves on the assumption you know what they are trying to tell you. Of course it was only seconds that had passed, when I finally said, "Why, what's happened?"

He then went on to tell me about a part of India that had declared independence, with the result that civil war had broken out. There were three European reporters being sent out and needed to have crews ready with them.

At least I could get a good night's sleep for we were booked to fly out from Belfast airport in the morning on a private charter aircraft. We would be heading for an American Air Force base in

Suffolk, where we would transfer to a military plane for the long haul eastward to a place I had never heard of. Dacca in East Pakistan! At this point, trivial things such as clothes and laundry arrangements didn't seem to be important.

I guessed the outward journey would not be a 'Cook's Tour'. The huge military aircraft was not intended for passenger comfort, so I could forget any ideas of sylph like girls coming along to ask what I would like from the trolley. There was a galley on board and it was manned by professional looking army chefs, but you had to serve yourself. As to my fellow travellers, two of the reporters I had already worked with, along with two cameramen, but other faces were unknown. There was also a group of diplomat types, who seemed to be constantly shadowed by what you could only call, 'heavies'. I later came to realise that they must have been part of some clandestine operation with politics at the centre of it all.

Where we finally touched down was a three hour drive from Dacca and after the briefest of security checks, we set off in a convoy of three up to date coaches. For the first two hours, nothing looked out of place. Yes, it was fairly barren and a little primitive where we passed through small communities, but we were in a part of the world where modern needs and technology had yet to find a footing. We were travelling in the second coach and perhaps by now we had become a little uninterested in our surroundings, when we were roused by the sound of rifle fire, followed by our driver swerving into the side of the road behind the leading coach.

Soldiers seemed to be everywhere and heavily armed. The driver shouted something to our local guide, who translated quickly, and told us we had reached a road block and may have to get out, but for now to stay calm. The 'suits', as we had now christened them, were travelling in the leading coach, and at the moment all the activity seemed to be there. We had been told before leaving the air base to keep all film cameras and equipment out of sight, save for one small 16mm mute camera that Peter had about him. As we sat trying to look calm, I heard him firing off a few frames of the scenes around us.

Now there was movement. Several high ranking officers appeared with three of the 'suits' and started to board our coach. It was a passport check, all done in silence until he came to me. I handed him my passport opened at the photograph which must have pleased him for he said, "I was at Cambridge some years ago. Do you know Cambridge? There is a Downing Street there also."

I had seen enough prisoner of war films to know that is how they trap you! All I could think to say was, "Really?" So long as he didn't ask the purpose of my visit, I thought I had got away with it.

For the remainder of the journey there was now a great deal of military activity. We were later to learn that some form of emblem had been attached to the leading coach, to give us a priority route into the city. From a distance could be seen columns of black smoke which indicated buildings on fire, all along the route was evidence of rioting with burnt out shells of cars on both sides of the road. Then we were halted again. This time the soldiers were not so high ranking, nor were they very smart. Our guide alighted and began conversing with them. Once again a feature film came into my mind, where a whole regiment was betrayed by a friendly guide. I heard Peter shooting more footage. It gave me a strange sort of feeling. I think it was fear. We were stopped again. This time it looked more serious. Soldiers, or maybe they were police, were controlling a crowd in a way that was bordering on barbaric. Sticks and batons were being used freely without remorse, giving no consideration to age or gender. It was the most sickening thing I had witnessed and by the gasps and utterances around me, I knew I was not alone. Once again, the 'Suits' came on board and one of them , trying to appear calm, but failing miserably, said from now on we would all have to travel in one coach. He went on to explain that the intended hotel was in an unsafe area and we were to be taken to a residence belonging to the American Government.

For practical reasons, all the crews and reporters moved to the rear, enabling the others to get aboard as quickly as possible. Or to put it another way, which one of the other recordists did, "Let's get the hell out of here." As we drove along, I made a mental note that all the 'suits' and 'heavies' were sitting nearest the only exit door. Strange how the mind wanders under stress. The residence was located in what was a more palatial part of the city. Nothing suggested it had any connection with America and there was no sign of any military guard. It was all strangely quiet.

But once inside we had an assurance that there was a western influence. The décor, the pictures and paintings on the walls, dominated by one of Richard M. Nixon and most of all the food on the table. The sleeping arrangements were limited but modestly decent and most of all the mattress was very comfortable. As I drifted in and out of a sleepy illusion, I thought I heard some distant explosions. The Europa Hotel in Belfast came into my mind.

In those milliseconds between sleeping and waking, I became aware of a bell ringing. I was unsure where I was. The light from the window was in an unfamiliar position, and then, reality. These were not familiar surroundings. The bell had stopped ringing, I heard a voice I recognised, I heard the word breakfast. There was movement nearby and Derek, my roommate was stirring.

"What time is it?" I asked.

"Dunno, God knows what the time difference is here."

As we spoke there was sporadic gun fire. Distant maybe, but a reminder that we were not covering army manoeuvres.

"Have you noticed it's not as warm as yesterday?" I said.

"Air conditioning mate," said Derek, adding cheekily, "You must be one of the newer boys!" This was a quote from the film, High Society, used by film crews, along with many other famous 'one liners'. Film crews, just like touring musicians used humour as a way of reducing tension in confined situations. Contrary to popular belief, film making involves a lot of standing around waiting for something to happen.

Breakfast was what you would call an all American clambake. Something to suit everyone's taste and in a very informal way. You just helped yourself. But it was to quickly become a briefing of the situation with the arrival of someone who introduced himself as representing the American Ambassador. What we had flown into was a civil war between supporters of a Sheikh Rahman, who had declared an Independent State of Bangladesh, and troops of the West Pakistan Government who were attempting to disarm them. In doing so, they were not distinguishing between civilians and Liberation Army separatists and so far, unconfirmed reports were putting the dead at 7000 in two ceaseless days of shelling.

The NBC representative was also on hand to try and formulate plans for film coverage. There were already two film crews, with reporters, who were temporarily marooned in the

Imperial Hotel in the centre of Dacca and while they could observe events in the surrounding streets, they had little chance of any filming.

At this stage it was unsure who the police were supporting. To have their protection in the streets could be dangerous if they were siding with the West Pakistan Army. The Ambassador's Representative had already suggested that many of the civilian deaths in the city were due to crossfire between both sides. There was a telephone link from the residence to the Imperial Hotel and it was possible to speak to the reporters, so with a little ingenuity and what three sound recordists had in their kit, it was going to be possible to file some kind of report. It had already been established that the television station was still transmitting, so therefore, their film processing laboratory must still be functioning. Furthermore, we had been assured that it was in a safe part of the city. All we needed now was to take the camera to the highest possible point and run off some footage to go with the telephoned report. It may have been a 'Heath Robinson' set up, but it was to provide some of the first 'on the spot' commentary to the Western World.

The local 'Fixer', who spoke good English and several Indian dialects, told us of the tragic scenes along the roads leading out of the city, as thousands of refugees tried to flee the conflict. He added, that by a roundabout route he could get us near enough for filming. Straws were drawn, (a most time honoured method of selection) and Derek and I had the short ones. By coincidence, both cameramen were called Peter. We set off in a Land Rover, which presumably, belonged to the American Government and wound our way through the streets. Ever conscious of trouble or someone with a rifle. We did pass several tanks without being challenged, along with squads of soldiers and again we were not asked to halt. There is one thing about a Land Rover. It does communicate an air of authority, which certainly made me feel a whole lot better.

We finally came up to a point where, across an open expanse of grassland, we could see people making their way out of the city. It was pitiful. Old and young alike. Some were leading animals, others had contraptions on wheels that held their worldly goods. Many of the elderly were transported in makeshift trolleys. They weren't shouting or chanting or complaining. Wherever they were heading could not be any worse than what they were leaving behind. To go any closer to film would have been indecent. Both cameramen used the end of the lens to obtain all the shots they needed. For Derek and I, it was just a matter of natural sound, although in reality, it was very unnatural.

On the return journey we found the route blocked by military vehicles, but 'Mr Fixer' knew a diversion, which although may have been a longer route, he thought it would be safer. He assured us by saying in his refined voice, "Apologies for the detour chaps, better to be safe than sorry, what!"

On the extreme outskirts of the city we came upon evidence of fierce fighting. There were wrecked vehicles, both civilian and military. Empty shell cases were scattered around what had obviously been a gun emplacement and the bodies of cattle littered the roadside. The whole area was being plundered by civilians trying to salvage something that might make their existence easier. They scattered as we approached. Trying to assure them that we were no threat would have been hopeless. After what they had witnessed in the last few days, any vehicle with an official appearance must have been a sign of danger. We rolled off some library footage, then beat a hasty retreat to the television station.

The NBC fixer was trying to arrange contact with the local Liberation Army Council. Messages were coming through that they thought their cause was being ignored by the west and in particular, by the United Nations. America had remained silent and yet here were we being flown halfway round the world and in residence at one of their 'safe' houses. One of the crews at the Imperial Hotel had filmed an interview with a leader of the group and this had been smuggled out to avoid being seized at the television station during processing. It was now time to take stock. Five crews was overkill now that the centre of Dacca was free of fighting and the Imperial Hotel was open for business again. Word came from London that the far eastern crews would cover the rest of the assignment and arrangements had been made to recall the three 'floating' crews. This would mean an early start from the residence to get to the airbase, but 'Mr Fixer', who was to drive us, didn't seem too perturbed. As he left us the night before departure, he called out, "Don't worry, we'll have a jolly fine show."

I have made no mention of the human carnage we witnessed during our stay, nor do I intend to elaborate. My fellow sound recordist, Derek, must have been of the same belief, for although our paths crossed several times over the next fifteen years or more, the subject was never mentioned. Meanwhile on the other side of the world! If that sounds like a line from an episode of Monty Python, it is intended to.

It may give some idea of the absurd world of television filming and the two extremes of stories. My first call was to travel to York to cover a story in the 'Ask Aspel' series. This related to ghost hunting but has no real connection with the purpose of the story. At the end of the first day's filming, we were relaxing in the hotel lounge and the subject of conjuring tricks came up. It was agreed that they were all sleight of hand or deceiving the eye, until Michael Aspel said, "I can do a card trick over the telephone and a voice will tell you your card." It was a conversation stopper if nothing else. He went on to explain that he would ask one of us to dial a London number, having selected a card. Then the voice would reveal the card. Spooky? Read on. There was a phone at the bar and the barman had a pack of cards. As I must have shown the most scepticism, Michael gave me a piece of paper with a London phone number to dial. I had already selected a card. Let's assume the seven of diamonds. The number began 01 which confirmed a London exchange.

I dialled the number then passed the phone to Michael and a few seconds later we heard him ask for a Mr Phantom. After a few words, he handed me the receiver and I listened to a voice tell me that my card was the seven of diamonds. It was very impressive and despite pleas for the rest of the evening to divulge how it worked, the best we could get out of him was, "Write your name and address on a five pound note and post it to me!"

Three years later, I met him at a BBC function at Pebble Mill, Birmingham and reminded him of the occasion he asked me to ring Mr Phantom, which he remembered. "You're going to ask me how it was done, aren't you?"

I replied by saying the thought never entered my head, but yes, how was it done? He then went on to explain, what is basically a very simple trick, but still very impressive when you are a long way from London.

It must have been 'Showbiz' month for the next assignment was to work with Morecambe and Wise, who had been booked to open a new clothing store in Leeds and the company, now the long forgotten name of 'Burton's Tailors', wanted a film record of the event. Comedians always say, when the crew are laughing you know it is funny and this proved to be the case on the first day. There were lots of behind the scenes routines that Eric and Ernie just 'ad libbed', before the actual opening ceremony. One of which concerned 'Miss Morecambe and Heysham' who was also along, as Eric put it, "To add some glamour and dignity to the event." The boys had worked out a little 'bit of business' for them to perform, where she would throw one liners at them and looked shocked at the replies. The trouble was, neither of the duo kept to the script, which confused the girl into fits of laughter and made the whole thing a funny event and not just the solemn cutting of a ribbon. A typical riposte went something like, "Do you go out very often?"

"No, not very."

"I've heard they call you the tide because you're out so often."

"No, no, I'm in a lot."

"So is the tide."

"But I sometimes walk my dog. He's eighteen years old."

"You should get a licence for him."

"No that would be a waste of money, he doesn't like TV!"

"That's a lovely perfume you're wearing."

"Yes, it's called Evening in Paris."

"Smell my jacket."

"What's that called?"

"Two fifteen in Darlington, but then it usually is."

The routine went on and on, to the delight of staff and gathered dignitaries.

We gathered in the executive dining room for lunch and once again, were able to sample Eric's rapier like wit at first hand. Ernie was recalling how he first started as a young boy in Leeds with his father going around halls and clubs doing a song and clog dance act. "We were known as Bert Carson and Kid," said Ernie.

"He was Bert Carson," quipped Eric. Another sample was after I gave him the feed line in an ordinary piece of conversation. I had ordered fish and was trying to sprinkle salt when the top came loose and spilled on the table.

I thought it was a natural thing to say: "I suppose I should throw it over my shoulder for luck."

Eric pounced and said, "No throw it over Ernie's. People will think it is dandruff and not a wig!" He never stopped clowning and had amazing energy, able to find humour in the most mundane of subjects. It was difficult to believe that three years earlier, he had suffered a massive heart attack.

During a break for coffee, I mentioned to Ernie about my interest in the cinemas and theatres of Leeds, which of course he knew well. I told him of my father's connection with the local cinema industry and how I had recorded his recollections from him starting in 1914. I then went on to ask if I could record some of his memories of those early days he had mentioned over lunch. Assuring him it was a purely personal interest and that I would be happy to let him have a copy. Ernie did have an interest in tape recording and used one for taping broadcasts and for rehearsing routines, so the idea appealed to him.

It was arranged for me to visit their hotel next morning before they checked out and being in good time, staff showed me into a private lounge. While waiting, I passed the time completing a crossword in the local paper, when in walked Eric, saw what I was doing and immediately said, "Rodscrows!"

I looked up and said, "Sorry."

Eric then explained it was an anagram of crossword.

"Not a lot of people know that," I replied.

"Not even Edward Heath would know that," said Eric.

Then Ernie walked in and said, "This is Ken, he's going to chronicle my doings."

"What he does in his private life has got nothing to do with me," joked Eric. I recorded around half an hour of Ernie reminiscing about his boyhood years. The tragedy was, although I did send a cassette copy to him, the tape copy was lost when my car was stolen while on location in Scotland.

All of this was a nice interlude before being booked by NBC to return to Belfast. However, this was interspersed with several days of rugby league stories with the much imitated, but much loved, Eddie Waring. The first time I worked with him, just before we were ready to roll, I asked him to say something just to obtain a level.

Eddie laughed and said, "You shouldn't have a problem with my voice." And he was right. It was the sort of voice recordists love to hear. All delivered at the same level. Unlike many voices which start low, then gradually increase. Or even worse. Those that start loud, driving the meter to a false level, then slowly taper away to almost a hoarse whisper. It was something that could not be taught in sound tuition.

Perhaps one more story about Eddie. The series of programmes on Rugby League were for the BBC. It was often their policy to send a trainee producer on location to give some idea of life away from the studio. This particular young hopeful was rather anxious to convey to Eddie that he had played a trial for his university, making it clear that he thought the only real rugby was the union code.

"Were you selected?" asked Eddie.

"Well not really," said the trainee. "My problem was, on the wing I could not pick up the passes. They said I would be better as a flanker."

"Are you sure that was the word they used?" replied Eddie.

The troubles in Northern Ireland had now spread to mainland Britain, with a number of serious bombings. One of them at Aldershot barracks was in retaliation for the tragic shootings in Londonderry, which, forever, will now be known as 'Bloody Sunday'. The demand for 'hard' news crews was growing and I seemed to find myself becoming embroiled in this grim form of television. But as dear old Les once said, "It's what sells newspapers."

The strange thing is, and I have found it so many times, that amongst all the turmoil and tragedy, there often is a lighter side. Sometimes it is apocryphal or based on hearsay, but probably true to a large degree. Two such stories to come out of the conflict in Northern Ireland concern Ian Paisley, a very dedicated and sincere man. You have to imagine the following delivered in that glorious forceful voice that became part of his persona.

During a particular period of the troubles, when both sides were indulging in retaliation killings, one reporter asked Mr Paisley, what he thought about the tit for tat murders? Mr Paisley's reply was, "I'll tell you what I think about it. It seems to me that there is too much tat and not enough tit!"

The second story needs a brief introduction to set the scene. In any radio broadcast studio, there is a standard question to obtain a sound level, where the reporter will ask the interviewee, "What did you have for breakfast?" It may also be used on location for the same purpose and as a way of relaxing the person about to be interviewed.

When Mr Paisley came up against this, he immediately thought it was a trick question and burst out with, "I'll tell you what I had for breakfast. I had a good Protestant breakfast of bacon and egg. None of your Fine Gael fish."

One day while in Belfast and just waiting for something to happen, as it frequently did, a Telex message came through for all reporters to be on call, along with crews for immediate transportation. Further details to follow. We knew that meant something big was about to happen. The news was not long in coming as the world started to hear that President Nixon had launched a series of bombing raids on North Vietnam. Once again there was a plan of saturation news coverage as the general feeling was that this would bring about an end to what had become a very long drawn out war for America. The attachment in Belfast at the time was two crews, along with reporters and fixers and we were given two days to prepare to fly out. At least there was time to attend to laundry needs! We flew out of Heathrow bound for Paris, where transport took us to a French military air base. From then on it was the American Air Force all the way.

Once again, the comfort was sparse but the food was excellent. I have always thought that all branches of the American military services did get their priorities right when dealing with the needs of personnel. It was daylight when we were informed that the aircraft was on final approach, although we were still twenty miles out of Da Nang airbase. We were flying above the cloud base and were accompanied by three F4 Phantom jets, who were our escort in case of attack by MIG fighters. We all felt very reassured, I think!

The landing was a rough one, either through severe winds off the mountains or maybe the skipper was feeling fatigued. We certainly were. On this trip, the aircraft was full of military people with some high ranking officers, who seemed quite nonplussed by being amongst 'other ranks' and film crews. However, on dispersal it was noticeable that 'other ranks', officers and film crews all had their own bus to ferry them to the various check in points on the base.

The check in was a rigorous one. After all we were in the middle of one of the worst military conflicts of the late Twentieth Century… This war had far outlasted anything the American Army had known and the casualties were still coming, as we were soon to witness. Da Nang base was huge, containing every possible requirement that a fighting force needed. Personnel were issued with a guide to help them find their way around. When I asked if we could have one as a souvenir, a big sergeant – and I mean big! – said, "What do ya think we're running here bud, Central Park!" We were shown to our quarters, a twelve bed billet. No problem for an old Royal Air Force hand like me, but frowned upon by most of the others. We comprised five cameramen and five recordists. The reporters and producers/fixers were next door. The one little touch of luxury though, we were collected at meal times and driven to the mess hall.

Next morning a planning meeting was organised to maximise the coverage for world networks. There were already three NBC crews working here on a basis of, two crews up country near the action, while the third crew stood down for two days. Now with a total of eight crews, the plan was to cover the war zone, plus in-depth features of life behind the fighting. In 'modern speak' the word would be logistics. Then it was known as forward planning. President Nixon and his Generals were convinced that the increased bombing would force the North Vietnam Government back to the conference table. History now shows it was nearly nine months later before a Peace Treaty was signed.

With Jim the reporter and Phil, my cameraman we set off to film some stories at the huge hospital complex. They were clearly intended for the home market, with each selected patient announcing his name and home town, then sending a brief message for his family. It was a morale booster for those back in the 'States' and also gave the troops a feeling that someone cared. The Army were very much behind the idea and provided all facilities, which included a vehicle and driver who was fascinated by the way Phil and I spoke. "It's the foist time I've heard real English spoken," he told us as we drove off.

Many of the seriously wounded were brought back to Da Nang after receiving superficial treatment at one of the field hospitals and the Army were keen to show this. It would mean a helicopter flight up country to see the medics at work and to help make the arrangements. We were joined by a Major who was nearing the end of his tour of duty. He carried with him a small 16mm camera, which he kept using whenever we were in the hospital wards. Traditionally, the cameraman is the senior technician on any film crew and I said to Phil that I was becoming irritated by the noise of the Major's camera.

"Tell him then," said Phil.

"You tell him, you're senior to me," I said.

"But you're older than me Guv and you were an SAC in the RAF," joked Phil.

I saw the funny side of his reply and burst out laughing. Remember, we were in a hospital ward with patients who had arms and legs raised in slings, swathed in bandages, tubes from nearly every orifice and coming over the radio, Cher was singing, "Gipsies, Tramps and Thieves."

The Major came running over. "Hey you guys, what gives? Let me in on it."

I told him we were worried about picking up the noise of his camera on the soundtrack. Then I added, "Washington may not be too happy." Whatever fear it provoked inside him, it did the trick. All his further filming was done after we were finished. The sights and sounds around the wards were depressing, but it was nothing compared with what we were about to see at the forward medic posts. Until then we tried to stay cheerful by amusing our Private First Class driver with variations in our lingo.

Sometimes we would break into rhyming slang such as, "Er, I'm in a bit of a two and eight over me plates."

Phil would reply with something like, "When I saw the look on yer boat I thought you must have a pain in yer New Delhi."

The young soldier was fascinated, I overheard him saying in the mess hall, "You should hear these guys, they speak real kookie."

Kookie or not, I bet he was glad he was the one sitting down to breakfast as we lifted off in a medivac 'Huey' helicopter to fly into the war zone. Phil didn't look too good. He had said to me earlier, "I could do without this." But I thought it may just be the early hour. He was certainly no 'greenhorn' when it came to action and he had been working for NBC since the Paris riots of 1968. There were four other helicopters flying with us, one of them, the Major informed us was a heavily armed gun ship acting as our escort. The Major had insisted we wear a certain amount of army style dress, assuring us it was only to help with identification. It did little for my confidence. I turned to Phil and asked him how he was feeling. If ever we needed a one liner from a film, now was the time. He came out with, "On the whole, I'd rather be in Philadelphia." This was the classic W.C. Fields self composed epitaph. I felt a whole lot better!

We were flying around three hundred metres above thick tree cover, when we were overtaken by a squadron of F4 Phantoms flying at a higher altitude. The Major shouted they were probably joining a bomber force to act as escort. The helicopter began to descend until we were at tree top height. Then a clearing appeared and we were quickly on the ground. The Major shouted that we could not stay long as we were in range of Viet rockets. If we wanted film action it had to be now, but quick. Somehow, Phil grabbed the camera and jumped out. In view of what was happening to him and what would become apparent in little more than an hour, he must have been in excruciating pain. We made our way towards two mobile field hospital units which were dealing with injured men on an almost conveyer belt process. The Major's presence ensured we were able to be close without impeding the medics and surgeons, who worked in totally unhygienic conditions, their faces blank and unmoved by what was happening all around. As if to add to the surreal conditions, a young soldier with horrific chest injuries raised his hand when he saw the camera, before he succumbed to the massive shot of Morphine he never felt being administered. All of this was accompanied by the cries of suffering and anguish plus the constant sound of helicopters either on the ground or overhead. The Major gave us the signal which meant we had to lift off. I took the camera from Phil, who now admitted he didn't feel too good, and helped him aboard.

Seconds later we were in the air and flying at tree top height. Another clearing came into view amongst the green foliage and as we hovered, we became shrouded in dust from the downdraft. As if by instinct, or more likely because he had done it so many times, the pilot just dropped the helicopter to a smooth landing. Again Phil climbed out first and I passed him the camera. We followed the Major to the edge of the clearing where I could see in the trees drums of fuel for the helicopters. My thoughts were it was an unwise place to be if you came under attack. The Major explained this was where serious amputations were carried out before being flown back to Da Nang. The Medivac helicopters could carry six stretchers, but in the case of amputees, this was usually restricted to three to speed the journey. "Can you get some of this action?" shouted the Major, just as a 'Huey' was lifting off. Phil began rolling and followed the helicopter as it rose quickly above the trees. A haze of dust already hung over the area, coating all the foliage with a strange effect of camouflage, but not hiding what was happening in the clearing. There was a distinct metallic crack, plainly heard over the noise of the rising helicopter. Suddenly there was shouting. An alarm whistle sounded. The helicopter's engine had stalled and it was nose diving into the trees some five hundred metres away. The next visible sign was a pall of black smoke rising from the crash site. I suddenly thought about the men who had just survived life saving amputations. And of the medics who were accompanying them back to hygienic medical care. It was the most sickening moment of my life and will remain with me all my days.

I looked across to where Phil had been standing and was shocked to find him lying over a packing case holding his groin. I shouted for the Major, who, like most other personnel had been distracted by the terrible crash. He came running over and gave a quick order to bring a stretcher. Two orderlies were on the scene, followed by a medical officer who gave Phil a precautionary injection. The Major outlined exactly who we were and our purpose to the doctor while he examined him for symptoms. I was able to confirm when he had first complained of the pain, also what his food intake had been. Whatever the injection contained had a soothing effect and Phil's face was now free from any discomfort. The bad news was, the medical officer suspected a burst appendix and he would need an operation at the earliest opportunity. It would mean an immediate return to Da Nang and as Phil had no say in the matter, he was lifted on the stretcher into the helicopter and we took off. As we headed south, one of the medics assured me that Phil would know nothing about the journey, which came as a relief. In a moment of nonsensical reverie, I had thought if only we were over Surrey and heading for a hospital in Guildford, Phil's home town. Then reality struck home. I was looking down on a muddy river that was slowly winding its way to the sea. The tree cover was thinning, there was some resemblance of farming, probably rice fields, where I could clearly see the people labouring away at some task or other.. Working for a bowl of rice a day had become a common saying at home, as a means of explaining the low cost of goods from the Far East.

We could see the base at Da Nang way off in the distance, which is hardly surprising as it covered close to 3000 acres. Nevertheless, it seemed an eternity before we were hovering above the pad close to the medical complex. An ambulance had been called to stand by and was ready to receive two stretchers, the other being a young GI who had contracted some form of fever. The Major helped me to carry the film equipment over to the hospital reception area and before leaving, left instructions with a nurse for me to be allowed access to the ward when news came through about Phil.

I waited over an hour before there was news. A senior nurse allowed me to lock the camera gear in her office, also providing precise details as to how to find my way through the maze of corridors to the ward. I arrived to find Phil in a separate annex and with him were two NBC reporters and a doctor. Phil seemed aware of what was going on, which was a relief. As I took his hand I knew by his grip that he was back with us 'big style'. It seemed a long time before he released his hold. The doctor told me the news. It was a swollen appendix, or 'grumbling' to use his terminology, but he may need an operation in a month or so if the treatment shows no improvement. Then Gene, the senior reporter added, "Thing is Ken, we're halving our coverage and as Phil can travel, four crews are outward bound from here tonight. How do you feel about being his 'nursemaid'?"

So that was it! I recalled Phil's quip about rather being in Philadelphia. Right now I would settle for Yorkshire, but there was the grind of the long flight, broken only by a refuelling stop at some remote base in Labrador or Greenland. As I was about to leave, Phil called out, "Is the gear all right?"

I was tempted to say something light hearted like, 'I've swopped it for some magic beans', but in view of what he had endured within, to say nothing about all the surrounding dangers, I just left it at, "Yes, it's fine."

I met up with the Major one more time. He had already made all the necessary flight arrangements. Laid on a vehicle to take Phil to the departure point and even gone out of his way to help me collect all the equipment from the hospital office. As he was leaving, I tried to find words to say more than just "Thank you." I was trying to avoid formality, but something more sincere than casual.

All he said was, "Ah forget it, that's what Uncle Sam pays me for. But if you're ever in Cleveland, Ohio, look me up." In 1995, I was in Cleveland, on holiday. By then I had forgotten his name and perhaps he had forgotten all about Vietnam.

The Lockheed C5 Galaxy lifted off from Da Nang just as the sun was dipping behind the hills. Army nurses had made Phil comfortable and he was in a mood to talk.

One of them asked, "How's he doing?"

I said, "He's talking."

"He'll soon be zonked after what I've given him."

I laughed and said, "Is zonked a new medical term?"

Without a flicker of humour, she came back with, "Yeh, it means zonked."

Phil enquired what had happened after the helicopter crash and I told him about him being strapped to a stretcher and then being flown back to Da Nang. He had no recollection of the trip.

*

It was almost like visiting hours at a hospital. He was reclining on pillows and I had to try and amuse him. I thought of the old chestnut about cheap air travel.

"Here, Phil, you've just started a new trend for Poundstretcher fares."

He looked at me and said, "I know the punch line, but give me it anyway."

And I came out with, "You can go anywhere in the world on a stretcher for a pound." He started to smile and was about to say something, but whatever the nurse had administered, it kicked in and sleep took over. It did leave him with a smile though.

*

It was finally over. We were now flying over English countryside. Phil was just about awake and taking in the surroundings, when a nurse slipped a thermometer in his mouth and took a pulse reading.

"You're doing fine; you've slept like a baby. We'll be landing soon," she said.

"Have we got an escort?" Phil enquired.

The nurse looked at me and said, "What's he mean?"

I told her it was an English joke.

"Oh, really, I've always wanted to meet an Englishman with a sense of humour." Our egos swelled, then as she was making sure the seat belts were in place, she added, "I'll just have to keep looking!"

I felt exhausted and in need of a rest. It had nothing to do with jet lag, although I suppose that was in there too. The sights I had witnessed already seemed like another world away, which made the Suffolk landscape look even more appealing as we touched down. Phil was taken to the military hospital on the air base, but was soon transferred to one near to his home. He made a complete recovery and to ensure there were no further problems, his appendix was removed. He never went back to hard news, but contented himself with local stories around the south of England, much of it being mute film. But we kept in touch for the next twenty years. I met his wife for the first time when I attended his funeral and when I told her how we had first met, she was surprised to hear about that part of his career. Phil had never spoken about it.

I suppose about two months passed before I took another assignment. There had been offers which, although not refusing, were steered in other directions on the pretext of already being booked. But it was back to normal with a job on the TIYL programme. For those who have not been paying attention, this was the code used by the production team of, 'This is your Life'. The setting was a quiet suburb in Manchester and the programme's victim was to be Barry Briggs, who was four times World Speedway Champion. The tribute was to be from long time friend, Michael Crawford, who was to appear to be riding a speedway machine through the streets of Manchester. Of course he was actually astride a machine on a trailer and we, the crew, were on the back of a lorry. The scene opened with Michael doing some stunts, then sitting down to deliver his tribute and ending with a shot from a side street showing the passing cavalcade of lorry and trailer with Michael and crew. It proved a popular insert too, as I would often ask ordinary people (Joe Public to TV journalists) what they thought of a particular episode of 'This is your Life', which always had good viewing figures. As of course did Michael Crawford as 'Frank Spencer'.

A more serious programme was set in an operating theatre, showing what the new developments were in major surgery. It was not for the faint hearted as much of it was in close up with the surgeon giving a commentary for each cut and probe he made. I have never understood the viewers taste for any programme set in a hospital. Because of hygiene, all the crew wore gowns and masks and in order to hear the surgeon, I had a boom swinger with a gun microphone over the action. As the operation was proceeding, I became aware of the sound rising and falling in level and looked up to see poor Roy looking as green as his gown, eyes closed and tottering on his heels with the boom passing to and fro above the operating table. With an almighty crash he fell amongst some chairs at the edge of the theatre. The surgeon, without even looking up said, "Pick that man up, somebody." There was little point in asking for a 'take two'!

The rest of the year was the usual mix of stories, as diverse as, an in-depth look at the life of Cyril Smith, who had just been elected MP for Rochdale. The programme was titled 'Larger than Life' for a good reason. Cyril was reputed to weigh 29 stones (400 lbs). Another story that was to run and run for some eighteen months was the investigation and eventual prosecution of the architect, John Poulson. This story was a real 'can of worms' from the beginning uncovering a trail of bribery and corruption. Resignations ranged from the Home Secretary, Reginald Maudling to countless company directors and councillors. It covered Nationalised Industries, Health Authorities and councils and was reputed to have involved over half a million pounds in bribes.

As Christmas neared, I received an invite from Les to spend a day in Lincolnshire. He had finished building a detached bungalow on a delightful plot of land and as you would expect, had made special provision for the hi-fi. On that particular Christmas Eve, the sound of a Wurlitzer or Gavioli organ could be heard played at a high volume across the surrounding fields. We took stock of our work load over the past year. Les was tiring of the weekly routine with BBC North. Aided, perhaps by two recent phone calls to work in Belfast. He decided not to renew his contract and to go 'freelance' again. 1973 might be a tough year for the more prestigious work, so it was decided to take anything that was offered, so long as it paid the rent (and lunches)! We were now both 'jobbing recordists'. 1972 did have one big disappointment though. Peter Handford had told me that he was starting work on Alfred Hitchcock's murder mystery 'Frenzy', which was being shot around London and asked if I would like to see the 'Master of Suspense' at work. I was all set to meet up with him, when Jim McKee offered me a week's work in Scotland which I could hardly refuse.

As they say, 'You never know what is around the corner'. Or as Les expressed it: "As one door closes, another slams in your face!"

In January I received two bookings for the same week. One with Border Television, the other in Dublin, working for RTE, which was a recommendation from NBC. We didn't know what the jobs were so the easy option was to spin a coin. I said, "heads", and won. I chose Border. This turned out to be a new game show entitled, 'Mr and Mrs'. It was unusual because it was shot entirely on location with no studio restrictions. The crew just turned up on the doorstep of selected married couples and Derek

Beatty went through his routine of questions about little irritating things in their marriage… To begin with, the programme was only seen by viewers in the Border Television region and HTV West.

I was working with my old buddy, Jim McKee. Jim had been there, done that and got the Tee shirt long before the expression was coined. And he had been very helpful in advancing my career with bookings and introductions into different areas of film sound. One of the occasions where he passed on work when he had a double booking was to provide a most unforgettable occurrence. One could say a 'Regal' event! This was with Grampian Television, working out of Aberdeen. Most of the work was local news and magazine type programmes, but one job was a visit to the Queen Mother's home at Castle Mey in Caithness to see her in residence. There were a number of restrictions laid down, to which the television company added some of their own. One of them insisted that all the girls had to wear skirts and on no account must trousers be worn. This had an amusing twist, for shortly after arrival and being introduced 'en masse' to the Queen Mother, one of the first things she said was , "You know, you girls should have worn trousers – it can get very cold here at this time of the year." One of my whims in life has always been epitaphs, the little one line endings on headstones. Here, I could add that I would like mine to be, "I had tea with the Queen Mother". But another could read, "I made the Queen Mother smile". Let me explain. We were sitting in a huge drawing room and the Queen Mother had around her, a Secretary, a Lady Companion and a Military Aide.

The Colonel was mocking army routines and phraseology with some amusing examples, then he turned to me and said, "I say, you are not recording any of this are you?"

I assured him I wasn't, but I asked if I could add an example from RAF procedure which was, "Beds will be made up, as laid down in Standing Orders." I can definitely say, the Queen Mother was amused!

During a quite spell (or resting as Thespians would say) I took the opportunity to expand my small record company. The Compact Cassette was becoming more popular with the advent of the music centre and now free of the constraints of the record pressing industry, I issued a number of titles which were aimed at the enthusiast market. I believe the term is 'niche marketing'. Much of the material was taken from recordings Les and I had made around the country while on location, or from public performances, sometimes the last occasion the organ was being played before the cinema closed for demolition or conversion to Bingo. Another pleasant interlude was working on a series of historical stories narrated by Alvar Lidell. His wonderful BBC voice, which began in the 1930s when news readers wore dinner jackets, was ideally suited to bringing a whole new meaning to past events.

As the year drew to a close there was more political unrest, with miners and workers in the power industry taking industrial action. The country had already been rocked by a doubling of petrol prices, as oil rich states began to take revenge for America's support for Israel during the Yom Kippur war.

At home, Edward Heath struggled to find a solution to end the industrial unrest, resulting in the country going on a three day working week to preserve coal and electricity. Periods of complete blackout lasting up to four hours were staggered for industry and domestic use. All television services closed down at ten thirty p.m. As the turmoil carried through into the New Year, both BBC and

ITV cut back on their programme outputs, which meant very little location film work. Reference to my work diary for the period shows a total of four working days up to March 8th. These were, two days on a BBC Playschool story, a news story about miner's picket lines and a look at how small industries were suffering due to the Three-Day Week. It gave me time to learn how to become a record producer!

In March there was a change of Government when Harold Wilson was elected. There were good times around the corner for the miners, for one of his first Acts was to concede to all their pay claims. For film crews, work began to increase, not only from London but in the regions where there was great consternation about the abolishing of a number of counties, plus the Ridings of Yorkshire, about which I was strongly opposed. Both Les and I were engaged on a series of programmes lamenting the loss of Cumberland, Rutland Huntingdon and Westmorland, which because of the locations involved, were a pleasant return to routine film work.

I cannot say the same about a job I was given to look at miners and the conditions they work in underground. The colliery was at Parkside, near Warrington in Lancashire and before being able to film below ground we had to obtain a camera and tape recorder that had been assessed as spark proof to comply with Coal Board regulations. Alan, the cameraman, and Kay, the reporter, joined me and a mining official in the riding cage. As he pressed the descent signal bell, he asked if this was the first time we had been underground. We all nodded in silence. "You'll find it interesting, they're shot firing today!" At this stage, that meant nothing to us. Then he continued: "It's nine hundred metres to the bottom before you ask!" At least it was brightly lit when we reached the bottom, but it was some distance to walk to get to a new seam that was just being started. Part of the way was reduced in height to no more than a metre, which meant hands and knees to reach the main chamber. My first thought was for Kay, but what a tough girl she proved to be, without any complaint she was through with the rest of us. Just as we arrived in the enlarged chamber there were two explosions and a large section of the roof fell in.

*

It would be foolish if I were to try and pass the experience off in a light-hearted way. It was terrifying and I was terrified. I cannot recall moments of past life flashing before me, but I, along with Alan and Kay were stunned. Until that is, we saw all the miners laughing at our alarm. It had been a controlled explosion all done for our benefit. Some twelve years later, I met up with Kay, who was now working at Central Television, Nottingham. Upon recognising each other, we almost said together, "Do you remember the day we went down a coal mine?"

Above ground there were some nice programmes to work on. One of the most enjoyable was a series on gardening presented by Geoff Smith. He was in charge of Harlow Carr Gardens near Harrogate and much of the filming was done there, which suited Geoff and myself also, being based only a few miles away. He was a wonderfully knowledgeable person and ready to help anyone who was having a problem in their garden, either with pests or merely trying to grow some particular plant. It was this guiding manner he had that gave me the idea of recording some of his tips for issue on cassette. He thought it would be an excellent way of helping the amateur gardener and roughed out some scripts which covered the four seasons, suggesting jobs that needed attending to week by week. They were all recorded in the grounds of Harlow Carr, to a natural backdrop of nature, pausing occasionally to allow jet planes from Leeming or Linton on Ouse to pass over.

There was still a mix of programmes with some old favourites such as Playschool and This is Your Life still helping to pay the bills. But there were also new names cropping up, such as Tomorow's World, Blue Peter and there was also an increase in work coming from the COI. This was the Central Office of Information, a Governmental department that was responsible for marketing and communications. One of their programmes which provided a great deal of work for freelance crews was TWIB. On this occasion it was not a code word to hide an identity, but merely stood for, This Week in Britain. The acronym being used because it was more convenient on clapperboards and log sheets. The stories could turn up anywhere and I worked on a number of programmes in Scotland, which enabled me to keep in touch with Jim Mckee. However, there was a wide variation in the stories. I recall one which took a look at the Scottish Opera Company rehearsing, plus events backstage with all the preparations to ensure a smooth performance. As was often the case, there were reporters covering English, Spanish and French versions. By way of contrast, one programme looked at all the gas that collected in a cow's stomach. Even going to the lengths of inserting plugs to try and draw off the vapour for possible recycled use. I wonder whatever became of the idea?

Another story for TWIB could only have been filmed in Scotland... It was about salmon and the amazing feat of nature that brings them back to their native spawning waters. Harold, the director thought the story could be shown to better effect if we had two boats in the middle of the river, giving, as he phrased it, 'a salmon's eye view'. The boats were delivered and the plan was that he would row out towing the second boat with David, the cameraman, and myself.

The PA girl would be with Harold. To save additional weight, we left our oars on the shore. David was muttering about the whole idea. We had worked together before and I knew he was a no nonsense type who would not tolerate these new breed of directors. He really was the last of the 'Movietone' age.

With a rope connecting the two boats, the progress was not rapid, nor was Harold very practical when it came to the art of rowing.

As we floated away from the bank, David came out with some of his quiet Scottish humour, when he said, "Look at him, he thinks he's Ernest Shackleton." For me it conjured an image from a schoolboy album about the explorer and I could recall a vivid pencil drawing of a line of boats all roped together and manned by at least eight sailors. We were trying to reach a weir to obtain close up shots of the salmon leaping, but at the moment we were in deep and slow flowing water. Across towards the opposite bank, the water was shallower and flowing quicker.

As he struggled with the oars, Harold shouted he could see hundreds of fish in the water. Each time he stood up and rocked the boat brought a shriek of fear from the PA, who was obviously becoming more nervous with each stroke. In his excitement at seeing all the fish around his boat, he accidently knocked one of the oars from its pivot and away it slipped into the water. All of which was accompanied by more screams from the girl as the boat rocked. David shouted for him to use the other oar to try and retrieve it, but by now it had floated out of reach. His attempts at trying to manoeuvre the boat with one oar were a dismal failure.

"I shall have to try and paddle," shouted Harold, as he began to imitate the Red Indian style.

"Now he thinks he is Nanook of the North," said David.

The forward progress was almost nil and we were still some two hundred metres from the weir.

Then Harold shouted, "I'm worried they will have all gone by the time we get there."

To which David replied, "At this rate we'll be in time to catch them coming back."

Harold, rather irritably, shouted, "If you can do any better, let me see you." The PA girl just sat petrified gripping both sides of the boat tightly, her clipboard and stopwatch were of no importance now. I shouted to Harold to try three paddles on one side, then change to three on the other. To his delight, it began to work and we started to move forward very slowly. He called out, "There are several dead ones over here."

To which David replied with, "They probably died of laughter after watching you."

"I heard that," called a breathless Harold.

We finally reached the weir after one or two more prickly exchanges between director and cameraman and came upon a most wonderful sight watching the salmon trying to clear another barrier in their journey up stream. Few made it at the first attempt, which brought out the poet in Harold as he sat quoting lines from Robert Burns and Robert the Bruce. The boats had now drifted together and I was able to see the girl was oblivious to the incredible act of nature that was happening all around. But at least the shrieking had stopped. For now!

David rolled off a full magazine of film before we realised that our angle to the weir had changed. We were in fact drifting, albeit slowly at first, towards the shallower fast flowing water. Trying to instruct the terrified girl to pull the rudder in the correct direction had no effect and Harold's frantic paddling resulted in our boat drifting in front of his. To cast off the rope would have left David and I marooned, then Harold announced that his plan was to head for the shallows.

"Then what?" asked David.

"Then we get as close as possible, although we may have to wade the last few steps," Harold replied.

The thought of wading threw the PA girl into a panic, imagining she would be waist deep in water. Harold patiently assured her that it was no more than fifteen centimetres, adding that he would get out first and pull the boat closer. David and I looked at each other with a lot less confidence. The progress was slow. Being tied by the rope allowed our boat to drift away from the direction Harold was making for. But to his credit, he did make it and his boat grounded in about the depth of water he had predicted. Furthermore, he began to pull our boat alongside which made for a stable platform from which to make our invasion of the river bank.

*

There was nothing for it but to take off shoes and socks and step over the side. David and I were encumbered with the equipment so could offer no help to anyone. It was perhaps only three metres to dry land, but the risk of dropping camera or recorder had to be avoided at all costs. Then it happened. After perhaps only two steps, the girl lost her footing and ended up sitting in the river, screaming loudly. Harold was the only one who could help and did his best to quell the tears. Running along the river bank was a public footpath and at that moment an elderly lady was passing with her dog.

"Exactly who might you all be?" she enquired. I was in no mood for explanations.

Harold was still trying to calm the distressed girl, so it was down to David to answer her query with, "Well we're not the Pilgrim Fathers, Madam!"

The sarcasm seemed lost on her, for she continued, "Have you been after salmon?"

Harold, now suspecting that she had us down as poachers, went on to explain that we had been filming the salmon leap for a documentary film.

But she persisted with, "Have you no got any fish in the boat?"

With a little more impatience, Harold came back with, "No, we have been filming the fish around the weir."

Quite calmly she replied. "Och! I only asked for your boats are away down the river."

We turned to find that, now without our weight, the buoyancy of the boats had risen enough to clear the stones and pebbles in the shallow water and were idly drifting towards the flowing current. Communication at this period was by public call box. The mobile phone was still a day dream in some far eastern scientist's mind, leaving the only option to enquire from the lady as to where the nearest telephone box was. To which Harold set off at a fast pace. Before we had embarked on our 'cruise', we had made arrangements with a river bailiff to be back at the departure point at a certain time, which was now approaching. Seeing his vehicle, we attempted a conversation across the river to explain our problem. He was able to reply with the news that, about four miles downstream there was a road bridge and he would make his way round to join us, while at the same time trying to locate the boats. It was close to half an hour before he joined us and heard our tale of woe, he was, however, able to report that he had located the boats caught up in some overhanging branches and was of the opinion that they would probably remain there. Meanwhile, Harold had been in contact with London, explaining that there may be the cost of two rowing boats to be added to the budget. He also had remembered the appointment with the bailiff, and had hired a taxi to take him to our starting point. When Harold arrived, he paid his taxi fare and started walking down to the water's edge where he was expecting to meet the bailiff. It was something of a shock to receive a shouted message saying the bailiff was on the other side of the river. However, he must have been greatly relieved to hear that the boats had been located. How to retrieve them was a different matter.

I only did one more job for the COI. Once again it was in Scotland, but this time in a stone quarry. It was intended to show the art of rock climbing and it was to be the first time I had worked with radio microphones, which were becoming favoured by directors for the freedom it gave the actors or reporters to move around at distances of a hundred or more metres from the camera. For this film we had a professional climber and a young girl reporter by the name of Emily who was making her debut in the world of films. The plan was for them to begin the climb with the expert explaining how the pitons and wedges are attached to the rockface. To climb a rock face she was, perhaps, just a kilogram or two overweight, but being eager to make an impression she faced the challenge with enthusiasm.

*

The professional climber, Andy, had used his experienced eye to judge an easy starting place and in very little time, they had both progressed to a height of around ten metres, even allowing for breaks while the camera was moved to change the shooting angle. I made mention of the use of radio microphones for the purpose of illustrating a strange misconception that became common amongst actors and reporters during the early years of their use, in so far as, they had the belief that when the director said 'cut', or the camera stopped turning for any reason, then their voices were not being transmitted. They may have been doubly assured by seeing the sound man had also stopped recording. Stopped recording maybe, but the miniature radio transmitters were still conveying every word to his headphones. As a light-hearted aside, I have often believed what a strong position a sound recordist could play in a blackmail plot after hearing some of the comments made during breaks in filming: criticism of directors' incompetence, or other actors' hammy performances – even amorous proposals between leading man or leading lady.

The most shocking conversation I heard, which for a number of weeks afterwards left me with a guilty conscience as to whether I should seek advice about notifying the authorities, involved two actors. They were playing a scene in a disused factory and by nature of the location, a number of breaks were needed to change camera angles. During a lengthy break, one of the actors was explaining a way of defrauding a travel agent and ending up with a free holiday.

But to return to the rock face and Andy and Emily. In between the breaks in filming, Andy had been very encouraging and by the time they had reached ten or so metres, he had found out her age, where she was born, the name of the hotel where she was staying and that she had no plans for the evening. They were now nearing the top of the climb and it only needed one more tricky procedure. Andy was in a position just above Emily and she had to make one final exertion to reach the last foothold. As she did, the top button of her jeans gave way and they began to slide down to her knees.

She had just delivered the line, "I can see the top." Now we could all see the bottom! Had the next scenes been filmed, they would, I'm sure have gone into the 'Funnies' hall of fame. Such a pity that YouTube was not around in 1974. In brief (pun intended) it involved Andy trying with one hand to pull her jeans up as Emily held tight to her hand holds. With no progress being made, Andy suggested some of his climbing colleagues should go to the top of the cliff and lower ropes down to secure them both. It was the easy option and with around seven or eight stocky climbers hauling on the ropes, the last few metres were accomplished without further mishap. Emily's modesty was saved with an over sized safety pin.

We were now heading for another General Election, the second this year and the work load was becoming very light. I had been selected for a short list of applicants to join the COI film department which would mean being London based again. Remembering my old instructor's advice about interviews and boards being good experience I accepted the offer to attend at a date to be arranged. In the meantime, by way of the film union employment lists, I had noted that a midlands based cameraman with an ITN News at Ten contract was looking for an experienced sound recordist. Little was I to know at this time, that in an obscure way, COI were to play a part in a change of direction for my career.

I travelled down to London to attend the interview, now being on a short list of three. There was also a reminder of my instructor's logic as all my travel expenses were being met. There were only three people sitting across the desk facing me and only one that asked any technical background questions. He was very much a civil servant in manner and appearance and I had noted that early in the interview he had established that I was a paid up member of the film technicians union. At the end as I was preparing to leave, he fired his final shot. If I was successful did I intend to keep up my union membership? I realised the answer would be the deciding factor and as I waited in reception for my cheque for expenses, I thought this will be my last contact with the COI. And so it proved to be.

As I was driving back to Yorkshire, passing through Leicestershire I noted the junction close to where the cameraman with the ITN contract lived. It was still early afternoon and as I was in no hurry, I thought why don't I find a public call box, ring him and arrange to meet. My next career change was about to start.

The man who started it all! Dad at the age of twenty-one in 1922 when working as a news cameraman for Pathé. He bought the negative for one penny per foot and Pathé paid him one shilling per foot for any stories used. As there were twelve pennies to a shilling, it seemed a good mark-up. The camera is a 35mm Williamson made in England around 1914. The photograph is a self-portrait and the quality of the negative is so sharp, it is possible – with magnification – to read the brass makers' plate.

Driving a Series 3 Nagra tape recorder for the first time in 1964. This was one of the Empire Reel Film productions which were shown as cinema programme fillers, also sent abroad to Commonwealth countries.

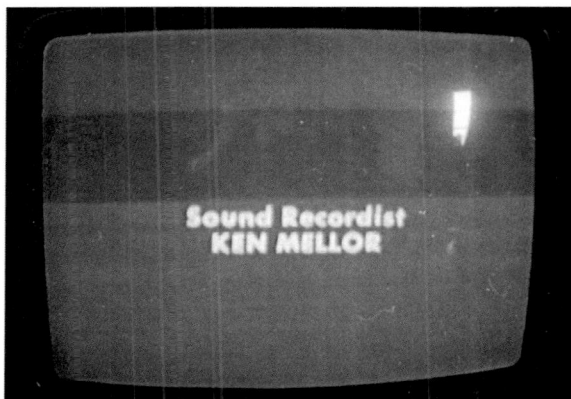

My first screen credit in 1965 – taken by Dad in a hurry on a cheap camera, but a lasting record nevertheless.

My tribute to Peter Handford – shown here on location in London for the film 'Frenzy' directed by Alfred Hitchcock, seen sitting to Peter's right. It was due to Peter's help that I was able to get a foothold in the film industry for which I shall always be grateful.

Eric and Ernie trying to be serious along with 'Miss Morecambe and Heysham' using Eric's theory of 'Dignity at all times'. Eric told me the story that they were going to call themselves 'Morecambe and Leeds' but it sounded too much like a day excursion.

The famous extra scene created by 'Lenny the Greek' at Hagley Hall.
Worcestershire. The background artists hardly strike a Seventeenth
Century pose, while the principle actors deliver their lines, having
taken a glance at the 'prompt' board along the way.

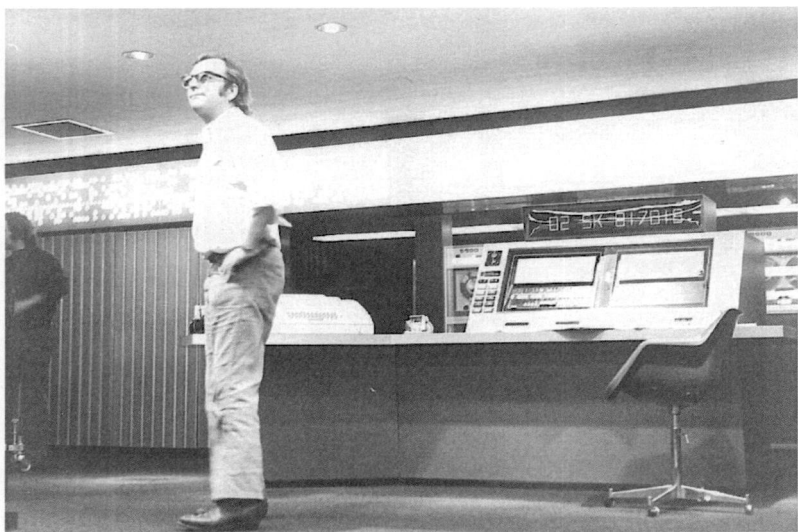

For anyone who holds Premium Bonds and has never won a prize (the author for one), this is ERNIE, the random number indicator that just sits in an ordinary room and whirrs away. The director, Richard Collin, is perhaps looking for inspiration for his next scene.

A roadside scene near Dhaka, Bangladesh. Live shells were scattered around being used as playthings by the children until the approach of our vehicle.

On approach to Da Nang Airbase in Vietnam, accompanied by Phanton F4 fighters. The war was on the other side of the mountains, but the airbase had suffered from raiding parties on several occasions.

A medical orderly guides a Medivac 'Huey' down into a clearing in Vietnam. This was a US Army nickname – the correct make being Bell UH-1 Iroquois

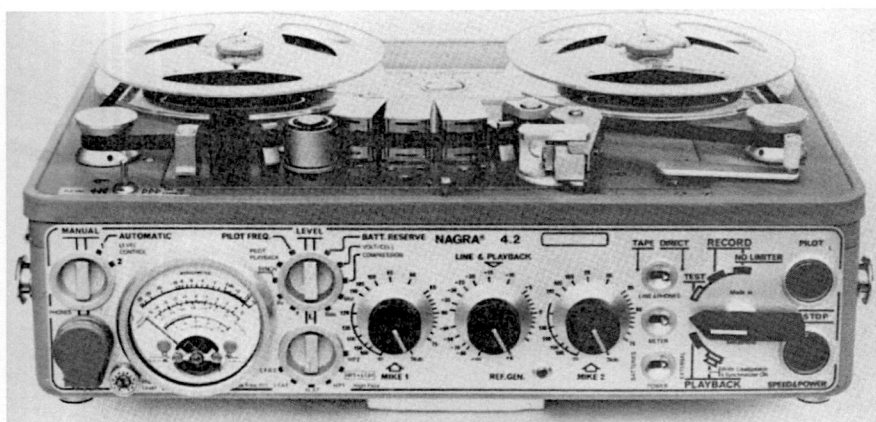

I replaced my Series 3 Nagra tape recorder with the updated version, Series 4. In 1972 this cost £630 at a time when the average house price in Britain was £7000.

A spoof with John Suchet. Having given him the camera and light and sound equipment, we then arranged with the National Union of Journalists' shop steward to call John to his office and discuss a rumour of him 'moonlighting'. Happily, John forgave us and we went on to work on many more stories.

All's fair in love, war and tea breaks! Complete coordination between rival channels during a house siege in Oxfordshire, where a child was being held at gunpoint. Refreshments were supplied by villagers during a five-day standoff.

'Out of the mouths of babies oft comes gems'. This young man had been chosen to act in the reconstruction of a brutal murder of a schoolboy while delivering newspapers. It seems he came across a robbery at a house and was shot at point blank range. Here, the young boy fights back the tears as he confides with reporter, Martyn Lewis, his feelings in retracing his friend's final footsteps.

A reunion in the Peak District – meeting up with Shaw Taylor fourteen years after he presented me with my film school certificate on the final night. Frank, too, was meeting him again for the first time in twelve years. This was the first of many Police Five programmes we did with Shaw on days when ITN did not need us.

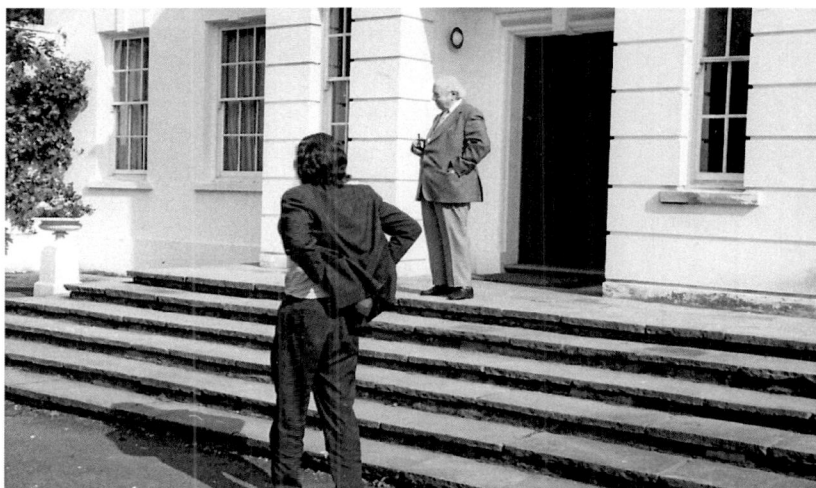

J.B. Priestly still trying to find out information about the programme to form his obituary, as we left his house. It had the delightful name of 'Kissing Tree House'.

THE BBC has made a virtual clean sweep of the Royal Television Society's news film awards—they will be announced on Sunday—but ITN has collected one : The film team award for the Grunwick demonstrations.

Embarrassment, however, has greeted the honour because, I am reliably informed, the film was taken by a freelance team and ITN are reluctant to let them steal the thunder. Instead, four names have been taken out of a hat.

Meanwhile more news of roistering, 44-year-old Reggie Bosanquet, who was complaining to me last week that the wine bar opposite ITN House closed down without so much as a by-his-leave.

Daily Mail columnist, Nigel Dempster, featured the story of our footage being denied the Royal Television Society's award due to internal politics at ITN. Just who leaked the story to him is now lost in the mists of time.

John Suchet emerges from the drain where the Black Panther had imprisoned Lesley Whittle. We had been in the complex of tunnels to stage a reconstruction of events which was shown as the lead story on News at Ten the day Donald Neilson was sentenced. It was John's first major news story with ITN and ran for nine minutes. After we had left, British Rail welded the manhole cover to prevent ghoulish sightseers from gaining entry.

Frank and I claimed to have flown in just about anything designed to fly, until the Goodyear Airship appeared in 1977. Having tried – and failed – to sell the story to ITN and ATV, we used a little subterfuge and took the camera along to the Goodyear press office and simply asked for a flight. They almost laid out a red carpet for us and we had nearly an hour of sailing through the sky: the only way to describe it.

The day we were arrested by PC Christopher Dean. Tory councillor, Jack Green, immediately contacted the local paper and told the story of the Labour councillor's attitude towards the press. It made the front page of the evening paper.

A publicity shot for the British distributor of the American Auricon camera when their new CP16 model was introduced. Frank and I were asked to assess its use and our verdict was favourable when compared to the German Arriflex/Rank system. Nick Gowing is the ITN reporter and in the background is a National Front demonstration.

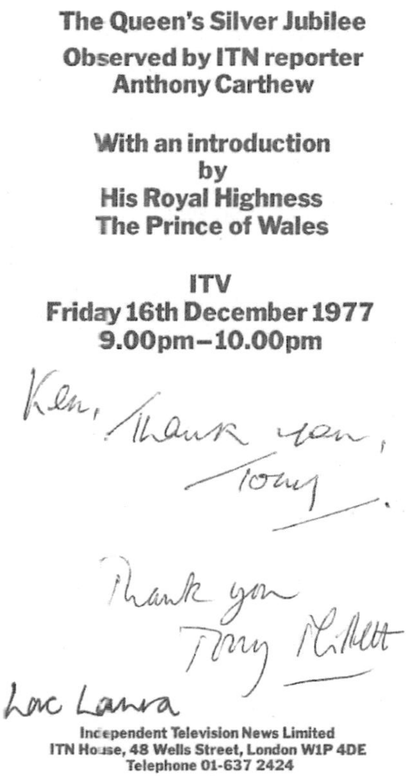

The Queen's Silver Jubilee

Observed by ITN reporter
Anthony Carthew

With an introduction
by
His Royal Highness
The Prince of Wales

ITV
Friday 16th December 1977
9.00pm—10.00pm

Ken, thank you,
Tony.

Thank you
Tony Rillett

Love Laura

Independent Television News Limited
ITN House, 48 Wells Street, London W1P 4DE
Telephone 01-637 2424

A 'Herogram' from reporter, producer, and secretary on the Queen's Silver Jubilee programme for our coverage of her tour of the Midlands.

Preparing to take a ride in a bosun's chair from the MV Decca Recorder to HMS Plymouth. The sea swell meant both decks were level on each high wave, resulting in a split-second timing for the transfer. Two cameras are visible, one being used in a tight close up on the explosion to destroy the sunken hull of the oil tanker.

An ocean-going tug battles against force 6 winds on the return to Stavanger. During our bout of 'Mal de Mer', Frank and I had made our way in near darkness to the rear of the vessel, giving no thought to the danger of being washed over the side. Health and Safety regulations were non-existent.

Skipper, lookout, and cabin boy. In the wheelhouse of the MV Nayland during our search for HMS Reclaim in the Irish Sea. Skipper Gordon scans the horizon while steering. Ken Rees is i/c binoculars. Above me is the speaker where we heard the message for all shipping to avoid a certain area.

Approaching hailing distance as we near HMS Reclaim in the search for the missing Tornado fighter. All under the watchful eyes of the Sea King helicopter and Top Brass on the bridge.

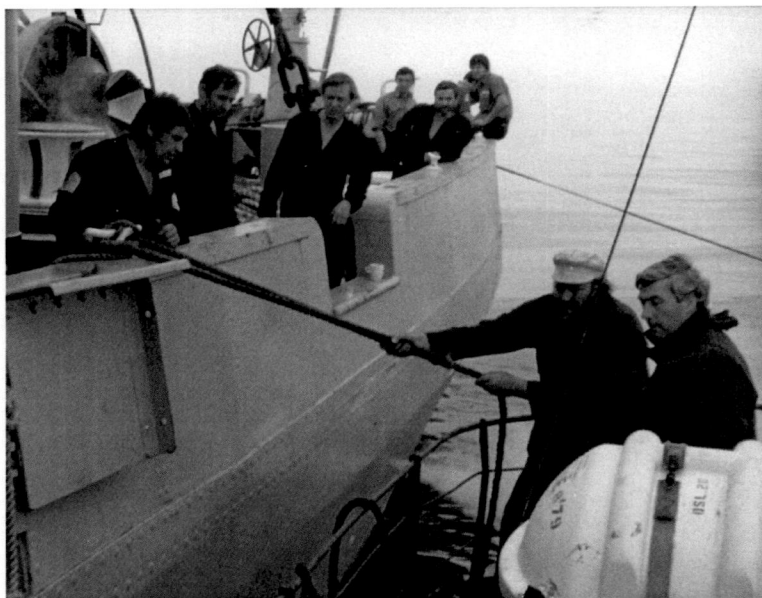

Tieing up alongside HMS Reclaim after being welcomed aboard. We are in the middle of the Irish Sea and it looks like a millpond compared with the gales of two days earlier.

Ever the practical joker, Frank set up this photo to send to the ITN Newsdesk after we had made the change from film to video – or Electronic News Gathering (ENG). The photo caption read, 'ITN Midlands ENG unit at the forefront of technology'.

Unfortunately we are not about to take a flight – just covering the arrival of British boxer, Henry Cooper, who had been invited to open a new theme park near East Midlands Airport.

A disaster story with a happy ending, proving that we really are a nation of animal lovers. This is Sefton, one of the surviving horses from the bomb explosion in Hyde Park where seven horses were killed. Sefton recovered from an eight-hour operation to remove shrapnel and became a mini TV star. Half his stable was taken up with gifts from viewers, ranging from mints to ginger biscuits.

The annual trip to the Chancellor of the Exchequer's garden before Budget Day. Nigel Lawson strolls with his wife and a young Nigella.

The late Terry Lloyd, soon after joining ITN, prepares for a "piece to camera outside Leicester Crown Court". Steve Riley checks the lighting (and hides the author) while Frank establishes a focus point.

Enough to give a modern day news editor apoplexy: a five-man crew on location a hundred miles from the newsdesk. From the right – Des Hamill rehearses his piece to camera, I check the level, Steve Riley fills in the shadows with a 'handbasher', Frank checks the focus and fixer, and Michael Crick takes it all in. Michael went on to be a founding member of Channel 4 News, later joining the BBC.

Before going into the operating theatre to film some explicit scenes in head surgery, we took time out to lighten up with 'one for the album'. Reporter, Sally Jones, worked for ATV but had been seconded to ITN for this story. And what a brave girl she proved to be.

Fun and games with John Cleese. He has just told Channel 4 Reporter, Jane Corbin, that all sound recordists are deaf! Much to her delight. The location is the Royal Station Hotel, Hull, where John was on location for the film 'Clockwise'. Also starring in the film was Alison Steadman, who we also interviewed – and both signed Frank's book.

Zola Budd tells me her version of the story about American favourite, Mary Decker, tripping over Zola's heels and leaving the track in tears during the 1984 Los Angeles Olympics.

The Battle of Orgreave: Hand to hand fighting took place before mounted police were called to drive the pickets back up the hill.

The Battle of Orgreave. Mounted police officers prepare to charge picket lines if loud hailer warnings to disperse are ignored. Frank has found a vantage point at a concrete post – extreme left.

The Battle of Orgreave: Mounted police make the first charge to disperse pickets and drive them away from the entrance to the coke works before the arrival of the lorry convoy.

The Battle of Orgreave: Police and crews are on what we called 'Rockobobo', or in plain language, keeping a watch for stones and missiles. During lulls in the rioting was a dangerous time when objects thrown from the back of the crowd were not easy to see.

The Battle of Orgreave: To a background of the coking plant, the daily
convoy of lorries arrive. On this occasion the police had cleared all
pickets from the entrance, allowing the lorries to enter without
stopping.

The Battle of Orgreave – *After the battle* would be a more correct caption. The date is 18 June, 1984 and future industrial historians may well relate that the miners lost their cause after this day. There were, however, another nine long months to go before a settlement was reached. An enlargement of this picture was featured in the foyer of ITN offices for several weeks.

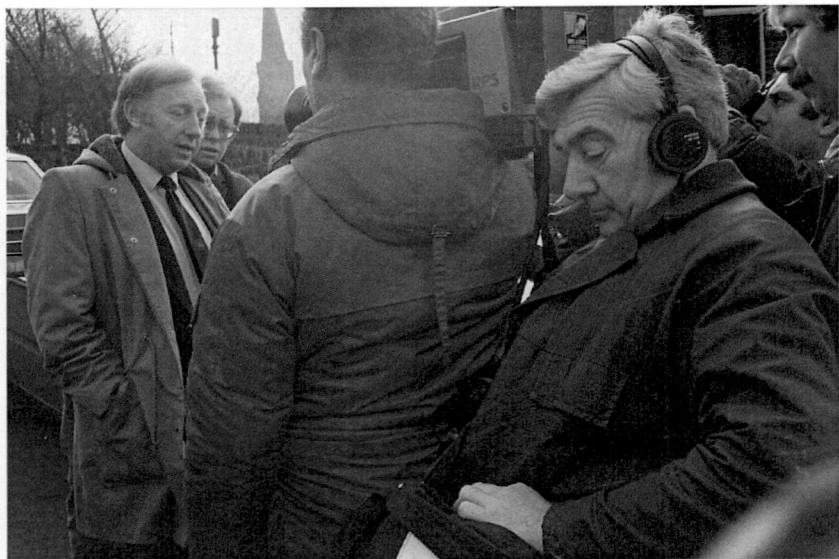

A very subdued and philosophical Arthur Scargill at the miners' Back To Work March at Cortonwood Pit, 6 March, 1985.

In the words of Del Boy Trotter, "It's good to be back on Terra Cotta" – after our hair raising flight over power stations and endangering the airspace of East Midlands Airport during the Miners' Strike.

End of Miners' Strike Party (I), in the coffee shop at the Grosvenor Hotel, Sheffield. *Left to right* – Russ, our lighting man; Frank; Ken Tebbenham, YTV sound; Rick Richards, YTV camera; and the author. The five of us had been the main crews during the opening weeks of the strike.

End of Miners' Strike Party (II): more fun and frolics. Left to right –
Frank Harding, camera; the author; Colin Baker, reporter; and Rick
Richards, YTV camera. Colin appears to have egg damage, while Ken
Tebbenham, YTV sound, keeps a wary eye on the knife.

The remains of the pumping house at Abbeystead, near Lancaster. Locals from the nearby village of St Michael on Wyre were on an evening visit to inspect the new installation. Methane gas is believed to have seeped into the site and it is thought the explosion was caused by an electrical appliance being switched on. Eight people were killed instantly and a further eight died afterwards from injuries.

One of the stories where we were being rested from the front line. I like this picture for a number of reasons. It shows a normal four-man news crew led by the late Jeremy Hands, who had been with us on many patrols during the miners' strike. Jeremy succumbed to some strange illness at the young age of forty-seven. On his left is Russ, our lighting man, and on my left is Frank, with the inevitable cigarette. The location is the Waterways Museum at Stoke Bruerne.

Another soft story we covered while on light duties behind the Miners' Strike battle lines was to film the re-emergence of Mardale Green in Cumbria. It was abandoned in 1935 when the valley was flooded to form Haweswater Reservoir. Frank and I are standing in the old village street.

Bradford Fire Disaster (I): Tributes started to arrive on the second day and in a very short time the whole area was covered by flowers, scarves, and mementos.

Bradford Fire Disaster (II): The stand where the blaze started from – nothing more than a discarded cigarette butt igniting years of paper rubbish under the wooden terraces.

Yet another illustration in the contrasts of stories covered. After spending a week on the Bradford Fire Disaster with 56 fatalities, our next story was straight to Alton Towers Theme Park. Here we were allowed to choose what rides to sample. The ITN reporter is Sam Hall.

It's nothing to do with us Guv! We were somewhere else. Trying to look innocent at a staged rail crash to test the strength of a nuclear flask for conveying waste material by rail.

Some of the hazardous jobs a recordist has to undertake – well, someone has to do it! You may ask what sound was there to record. It came from the enthusiastic photographer with calls such as "Pout baby", "Toss your head, sweetie", and "Give me that look, honey".

Caught in the act of being a record producer during one of my sabbatical breaks. The occasion was a recording of the organ at the Regal Cinema, Henley on Thames, played by William Davies. (John Foskett)

Deputy Prime Minister, Roy Hattersley, turns reporter for a piece about his constituency in Birmingham. ITN reporter, Ian Glover James, oversees the story.

In the 'press pen' at the Old Bailey on the day of the release of the Birmingham Six. Paul Hunt is right of camera; author on the left. (Joanne O'Brien)

I was never a devout football fan, but Brian Clough was one man who made it sound like a game of two halves. This was the last time I worked with him on a documentary called 'Goodbye to Cloughie'. Forty years in the game had taken its toll on him and he was only fifty-eight and not in the best of health. (Paul Hunt)

Miss Loren wearing the blouse that cost 800 francs in Paris, although she is not laughing at the joke I made about it. The incident I mention came about later and she can be forgiven for not seeing the joke. She had, after all, been keeping that smile fixed for over an hour. While she was in Britain publicising her book she also made the film 'Firepower', directed by Michael Winner. (Copyright Mirrorpix)

Mrs Thatcher was not in residence at the time, but Frank, ever the practical joker, wanted to have some Christmas cards made with the caption from Stevie Wonder's hit song, 'I Just Called To Say I Love You'. Fortunately, his better judgement prevailed.

A sad reunion of sound recordists on the occasion of Frank Harding's funeral. On the left is Roger Cowper who was his first recordist at ATV in 1960. I was his last. Roger's wife, Vicky, is on the right, while appearing between us is former ATV reporter, John Mitchell.

CHAPTER FOUR

THE ITN YEARS

The man I was about to meet was Frank Harding, an inveterate cameraman who had started his career in 1957 with the beginning of commercial television in the midlands. He was a news cameraman with a tough background, for he had survived two air crashes. The first as a teenager in a Wellington bomber which clipped some trees while coming in to land. The second time in an RAF Whirlwind helicopter after an engine failure over forests on the Welsh border.

We had a great deal in common. And yet we were as unlike as chalk and cheese in so many other ways which may well have been the secret of a working relationship that was to extend over a period of twenty years. At the time I was thinking of something on a more temporary basis, perhaps until the country's economy began to improve and work prospects would broaden again to the opportunities and variety of stories and programmes of previous years. Frank explained about his link with ITN. It had begun during the Paris riots of 1968 when he supplied much of the footage that was transmitted by ITN in Britain and was to continue back home with coverage of any major stories in the midlands area. He had also been out in Zambia setting up their first television service under the then President, Kenneth Kaunda.

ITN had established their first regional office in Manchester in 1970 and with a reporter and crew in the area, were able to give a wider coverage to stories rather than having to rely on the local ITV stations. They were now looking to create a sound crew in the midlands and as there was a rapid rail connection between Euston and Birmingham, this would enable London based reporters to be used. Frank continued to outline the agreement which included a generous daily rate of pay plus an allowance for equipment and realistic meal allowances, it did, however, mean being on call at any time, or in modern parlance 24/7. The only other condition was being based in the area. The midlands crew tag was to become something of a misnomer, for as we steadily turned in more and more lead stories, the boundaries were being stretched to Edinburgh in the north and Cardiff in the south. Or as Frank liked to claim, 'from Yarmouth to Barmouth'.

So that was all there was to it. We shook hands and I went off to await the first call, never stopping to think about that little piece of advice Shaw Taylor had left us with some ten years earlier regarding verbal contracts! Without trying to be too flippant, I could say that things got off with a bang! The first story was a call to Birmingham to cover the pub bomb blasts caused by two devices exploded simultaneously at the Mulberry Bush and the Tavern in the Town, bringing down tons of rubble onto crowded bars. Up to this date, it was the worst terrorist outrage on the British mainland. Seventeen people were killed and well over a hundred were injured as passers by helped with the rescue. Private cars and taxis were used in addition to the fleet of ambulances to take injured customers to hospital.

A few days later six men were arrested and charged on what was later defined as doubtful evidence and which was to start a long drawn out campaign to free them. It was in fact seventeen years later that I stood outside the Old Bailey working with the BBC, when racing from the Cheltenham Festival was interrupted to bring live coverage of the six men walking free from the court. Prior to that I had also worked on two documentaries covering each man's case history, from early life in Belfast to arrival in England and their search for work. But all of this was in the future. The reality on that November night was the carnage brought upon all of the innocent young people enjoying a quiet after work drink.

This story led all bulletins for several days which at this period were the one p.m. 'First Report' fronted by Robert Kee, followed by the five forty-five p.m. 'Early Evening News', then came the flagship programme 'News at Ten', with Alister Burnett and Reginald Bosunquet. Other familiar ITN faces reading the news in this early 1970s period were, Gordon Honeycombe, Sandy Gall, Andrew Gardner and Leonard Parkin. It certainly proved to the ITN Newsdesk that a midlands based crew had its usefulness. As did another midland's story some two months later, which was to run for over a year.

This was the abduction of the seventeen year old heiress, Lesley Whittle, who was taken from her home in Shropshire in the middle of the night in a most brazen kidnap plot by a man who was to become known as the Black Panther. It started a huge police manhunt, not only across the midlands, but as far away as Lancashire and Yorkshire, when it was found that bullets that killed a West Midlands security guard were matched with those that had been fired in a Post Office robbery.

It was a story that was fraught with confusion between neighbouring police forces, misread clues, a botched ransom drop and resentment that led to the near persecution of one of the West Midlands senior detectives. Each day's press conference would bring some more clues as the police tried to maintain a maximum of press coverage, to such an extent, that both newspapers and television were leading the hunt at a number of locations.

A cassette recording had been sent as part of the ransom demand, and this led detectives to an area near Kidsgrove, in Staffordshire where there was a large complex of drainage tunnels at a point where a canal and a main line railway passed beneath Harecastle Hill. In earlier years the canal tunnel had been replaced, leaving the original running alongside, although it was now badly silted with deep mud. Just who came up with the idea, I have long forgotten. It may well have been our intrepid reporter, the late Keith Hatfield, who was usually game for a challenge. He found a local joiner who would make us some lightweight wooden battens similar to arctic snowshoes in the hope that this would allow us to walk on the mud and enter the tunnel. The idea was to try and gain access into the labyrinth of tunnels.

We progressed to around fifteen metres aided by a battery light from Jack, our lighting man. Up ahead we could make out a second side passage that was draining water into our tunnel, with the result that the thick mud was now turning into a slurry which would no longer support the wooden shoes. Even Frank said he thought it was becoming dangerous. What we did not know at this stage was that we were only metres from the girl's body. This was discovered by the police three days later, it being a total of fifty two days since she had been so brutally seized from her bed. But it was not to be the end of our underground explorations. Sixteen months later, we would be entering the tunnel where the girl had been held prisoner as part of a reconstruction for News at Ten, following the sentencing of Donald Neilson on five charges of murder. In addition to Lesley Whittle, he had also murdered four people in Post Office raids. By a strange quirk in our law, a shot security guard had survived for more than a year and a day, so making a charge of murder unanswerable. Prior to this we had been involved in several false stories of his arrest, often being called out during the night if police had made an arrest after a robbery and of course there were the inevitable admissions by that section of the community who delight in owning up to major crime stories. As 1975 grew to a close the story had long been out of the headlines. Now it was the car industry that dominated the bulletins. The future of Chrysler. The future of British Leyland. The future of SU Carburettors. It was on such a story in December that we arrived at a factory in West Bromwich, the angle being that as a supplier of components to the car industry, their business was being badly affected and the next stage would probably have to be laying off some of the workforce. We were due to meet Martyn Lewis. It had now become quite common for him to cover stories in the north of England as well as the midlands, and as we were preparing to interview one of the directors against a background of inactive vehicles and fork lift trucks, a secretary appeared, saying there was a call for Martyn and would he ring his London office.

When he reappeared, it was quite obvious by the look on his face that some big story had broken. All he said was, "Pack the gear, forget this story, we have to get to Mansfield pronto, the police have arrested the Black Panther." It was slightly embarrassing because the factory owners had laid on a mini banquet by way of a gesture of thanks for their expected nationwide publicity. With hasty apologies being called, we made a rapid getaway towards the motorway to start a fast journey to Mansfield, while at the same time keeping a wary eye on the rear view mirror!

When we arrived at the police station, the media circus was already gathering. The men everyone wanted to speak to were the two miners by the name of Roy Morris and Keith Wood, who had assisted two constables in overpowering Neilson after he had held them at gunpoint in a police patrol car. They had stopped him in the early hours, walking along a road carrying a holdall and when challenged, he had produced a shotgun and ordered them into the car. They had managed, by violent swerving to throw him off balance, although the gun did go off and they finished up on the pavement outside the shop where Roy and Keith were waiting. The two PCs screamed for help as they tried to overpower Neilson and the two miners acted by first, Wood delivering a Karate chop to the neck and Morris landing a blow that totally subdued him, allowing PC White to snap on handcuffs. He was then further handcuffed to iron railings while they called for back-up, still not realising they had caught the most wanted man in the UK.

It turned into a long day of interviews with our material leading the early evening news and News at Ten. The interviews continued the next day as police gave out more background details and praised the public for their co-operation in bringing about an arrest. They also gave details of the many hours of complicated police work that had been involved and the diligent work of Scotland Yard officers. However, the one man that the press wanted to speak to, Chief Superintendent Bob Booth, summed it up with what he had maintained all along. That it would take

'Good honest simple coppering to bring about a result.' In view of the way he had been treated, it was an accurate statement. 1976 became known as 'the year of the drought' with what seemed to be never ending stories of empty reservoirs and dried up river courses. It was also a period when English football supporters were creating mayhem at home and abroad, which did little to help the image of the sport. Blame was placed at various doors from managers to a lowering of Government attitudes to violence, with the police in the middle trying to maintain law and order. It was not only in sport that there was dissatisfaction with one's lot. The prison service had a number of disturbances to deal with. One large scale riot occurred at Hull Prison to which we were called in the early hours and faced a two hour drive, so we knew it was going to be a long day. We had by now amassed our own library of A to Z guides covering all the towns and cities which we thought would fall within our patch, so arriving in the immediate area of the prison presented no problems. Our reporter, Martyn Lewis, was already on the scene and had found that the only vantage point that gave views of the jail and the prisoners out on the roof, was from a block of flats near the perimeter wall. On one of the balconies, some women were in voice contact with the rioters about which the police and prison authorities could do little, but photographers knew it was the only place they could obtain any pictures. The police, however, had barricaded both ends of the street to prevent access to all accept residents. It was going to take more than nerve to crack this one!

The answer came when we saw the local milkman was using a battery operated float for his deliveries. A proposal was made to him and with the help of some 'rustling' money, he agreed to carry the camera and recording gear to the entrance of the flats. He also gave us the layout at the rear and how we could reach it from our position and assured us he would let the girls know what was happening. Frank didn't see this was a problem as he was convinced they were 'Ladies of the night'! As for me I was prepared to give them the benefit of the doubt.

The equipment was hidden under some egg boxes and as the milkman was under no suspicion, there was no reason for him to be stopped. Our progress was not quite as easy. It involved climbing through a derelict building, scaling a medium sized wall, aided by some conveniently abandoned packing cases and pushing aside a redundant three piece suite. When we emerged into the street we were still at least fifty metres from the entrance to the flats. My mind wandered to the tunnellers in the film, The Great Escape, who, after six months of digging came up short of the boundary wire. Luck had failed us too. Where we came out, three policemen were coming up the street and started to give chase. Frank and I made it into the flats, Martyn was not so fleet of foot. He was apprehended and frog marched down the street. As we looked down we heard him call out, "I will alert ITN."

It was the ideal position for pictures and we were also able to feed some questions to the prisoners through the women as to what their demands were. How long were they prepared to hold out? And what the conditions were like inside the cells. It was the best we could do without a reporter.

There was also another problem to consider. We had all this footage that no other crew knew about, but we were fifty miles from the processing laboratories in Leeds and it was three hours to the lunchtime news at one p.m.

There was a telephone in the flat which seemed to ring at regular intervals, so maybe Frank was right! However, we took control of it to contact the London Newsdesk and advise them of the material we had and that we needed a despatch rider to convey the film to Leeds. There would also be a film editor to be put on standby and transmission lines to be booked for the Tele Cine. The final act in the plot was to persuade one of the girls to carry two cans of film past the police barricade and meet up with the courier two streets away. Amazingly, it all worked and we were able to watch our film leading the lunchtime headlines, while we were served with mugs of tea and the thickest corn beef sandwiches I had ever seen. Domestic catering was obviously not these girl's strongpoint. I became convinced that Frank was right after all!

I, like many other film technicians, tended to identify individual years with major events. There had already been the IRA year, the Panther year, the Drought year, now, for 1977 we would have the Jubilee year when Her Majesty Queen Elizabeth would celebrate her Silver Jubilee. Anthony Carthew was ITN's Royal Correspondent and we were selected to cover all the events and functions across the midlands. This meant receiving clearance from the Scotland Yard Press Office to obtain Royal Rota passes along with an identity card, which in later years was to serve as a Passport to gain entry back into Britain.

Other notable events during the year ranged from meeting up with Shaw Taylor on a Police Five programme which he presented on ATV in the midlands, the first of many meetings with controversial football manager, Brian Clough, a number of stories following the death of Elvis Presley and coverage of a long running industrial dispute in West London. This resulted in our film winning the News Story of the Year Award, but we were denied any glory due to internal politics at ITN, about which I shall explain later.

To meet up with Shaw Taylor after almost fifteen years was a pleasant occasion for both myself and Frank. Shaw had started at ATV in 1957 at the same time as Frank joined the camera department and we were to go on and make many more programmes with him. This also led to us both being hired to the ATV News Desk on the days when ITN had no occasion to use us, which in turn led me to meet up and work with a lighting cameraman I had first met back in 1964. This was Harry Oaks from the world of feature films and special effects who enjoyed the cut and thrust of television news as a way of relaxation away from big screen productions. Harry's credits were long, but included such titles as 'Superman', 'Flash Gordon', 'Memphis Belle', 'Quatermass' and many episodes of the Gerry Anderson classic, 'Thunderbirds'. His early career had included war service with the Army Film Unit which included the horrific scenes during the liberation of Belsen Concentration Camp.

Brian Clough was a charismatic figure amongst football managers and he did not suffer fools gladly. There is a long line of reporters who have suffered his wroth for daring to step out of line once he had made his point. He was, however, kinder to film crews, knowing they had a job to do and that they were only there on a whim from some news editor. Frank and I found favour with him from our first meeting. All because of Frank's book! Perhaps I should at this stage explain what it was for, I shall refer to it in later pages. It resembled a hotel register where guests could sign in with a date, name and a comment and had been in use from when Frank first joined television. It always created interest from anyone who was asked to sign in, if only to look back at some of the 'star' names and the comments they had written. Some of the early signatures were, Bob Hope, Paul Robeson, Eric Porter, Richard Burton, Harold Macmillain and the entire cast of the first series of Crossroads! 'Cloughie', as he came to be known as, was keen to sign, adding his favourite saying, "Be good young man". But I also found favour with him when I told him my Grandfather had been the manager at the Regal Cinema in West Hartlepool. This was where Brian and his wife, Barbara, had done their courting and as he had begun his managerial career at Hartlepool United he had happy memories of the town. So Frank and I could do no wrong and that was the case when one morning we had been instructed to turn up at Nottingham Forest ground to await a reporter who was travelling up from London. It was some story over a transfer and Mr Clough was being tight lipped. When he saw us and found out the purpose of our visit he made it clear that he would make no comment, but he said he would get someone to make us tea and we could sit in the outer office.

In due course a taxi arrived and out stepped John Suchet to try and obtain an interview. Brian came out of his office, looked John up and down and then turned to us and said, "Is this what you have been waiting for?" Then he turned and walked off to join the players. And that was that. No interview. No reason why. All we could do was drive John back to the station to catch the next London train.

News at Ten had become a very popular news programme which drew high viewing figures. The two man newscaster format had set new standards for television journalism and to round off the programme each night a tail end story was introduced under the heading, 'And finally'. These were always soft stories, usually ranging from the sublime to the ridiculous, but always tinged with humour.

When the death of Elvis Presley was announced, news agencies around the country were quick to submit some rather weird stories of how some fans were expressing their distress.

We were sent to cover three stories around the midlands, the first being in Leicester where we came upon a small terrace house that had been turned into a shrine. Every window and door featured Elvis. He looked up at you from floor mats, he stared at you from wallpaper patterns, he even played a part in the smallest room in the house! Every National daily newspaper had been bought and ironed flat to remove any creases. But the final homage to his passing was the householder applying to the telephone company to change his number to that of Elvis's date of birth. We followed this by visiting the home of someone who had made a life sized image in plasticine, using all the colours of a typical Elvis stage costume. This was a poorly researched story as the sculptor had a very pronounced stammer who, sadly, was unable to describe his monument for television viewers.

On the following Sunday, an Elvis Appreciation Society from Birmingham booked a little church in a Warwickshire village to hold a remembrance service, substituting Elvis hit records for hymns. My endearing memory of the day, in addition to seeing rock and roll in the aisles, was to hear the ageing vicar announce that, "The congregation will now sing Do Not Step on my Blue Suede Shoes."

An example of how flexible the midlands crew had become can be shown by two stories at the opposite ends of the news spectrum. We were booked to travel to North Wales to join Martyn Lewis at Porthmadog to spend a day on the Ffestiniog

Railway. This was one of several narrow gauge railways that had been restored by enthusiasts and was now becoming one of the top tourist attractions in the area. It was a glorious summer's day making a perfect picture and sound story, and we even achieved every schoolboy's dream by driving a steam locomotive.

On our return to Porthmadog, we made the usual check call to London as we prepared for a long drive home. But we were given instructions to make our way to Cardiff to join a coach load of miners who were planning to drive through the night to support pickets at an industrial strike in West London. This was a long running dispute at a film processing plant known as Grunwick and had begun when the management had refused to recognise any trade union within the factory. The coach with the miners was due to leave Cardiff at two a.m. so we had time for a leisurely meal before setting out. What we did not realise was that petrol stations were not only thin on the ground in North and Mid Wales, but tended to close around six p.m. and as our route finder showed a distance of 160 miles, the situation was tricky to say the least. After around fifty miles we took every opportunity to coast on favourable downhill stretches, but by the time we had travelled 100 miles we were beginning to think the car was running on just fumes.

We still had around fifty miles to cover, when, as we were driving through some small unpronounceable village, we noticed a police car outside a police post and decided this was our only hope. He was sitting alone filling in some paperwork when we told him our plight. All he said was he knew where he could get a couple of gallons and to give him twenty minutes. He came back with two cans and a funnel to assist in the decanting and we were soon on our way after gratefully paying above the normal retail price. Where he obtained it we didn't care but we suspected there was a blue panda car that we had to be thankful to!

We arrived at the Grunwick factory around six a.m. and met up with ITN reporter, Des Hamill. There was already trouble from groups who were not connected to the factory and were merely using this as a platform for their own politics. We had also gleaned from miners on the coach, that there was a plan to attack the coaches that were ferrying workers into the factory.

Des was happy to leave it to us in the restricted area around the entrance and there was just room for the two of us on a low gate house roof. The police tried to protect the first coach to arrive by surrounding it with officers on both sides, but came under attack from, first bottles and stones, then a mass push by hundreds of pickets. This was possibly the first time that mass picketing had been used during strike action in Britain and on this occasion was made up from large numbers of miners from the Yorkshire coal field, along with those that we had travelled with from South Wales. Violence broke out everywhere around our position and at first it seemed that the police may be outnumbered, until waiting reinforcements came in and completely surrounded the pickets by forcing them in to a confined area and picking out the ring leaders. The prize arrest, which happened just a few metres below us was that of Yorkshire miner's leader, Arthur Scargill, who at first refused to go quietly until sheer numbers of officers persuaded him otherwise. The humiliation for him and many other pickets around him took away much of the force of their attack and the police finally gained control of the road, allowing the coaches to enter the factory.

By lunchtime the crowd had dwindled to three or four small groups, easily contained by the police on duty so we were given a stand down order from ITN and headed for Paddington Station and a train for Cardiff. It was another warm day and we were both asleep by the time the train was passing Slough. I remember waking in complete darkness until I realised we were passing through the Severn Tunnel, but there was around a three hour drive even after arrival at Cardiff so we were still a long way from a comfortable bed. Maybe it was the thought of all the overtime that kept us going.

When October came and we read that the Grunwick coverage was to be entered in the Royal Television Society's News Film Awards it seemed that all the long hours had been worthwhile. However, it was not to be. Somewhere in the inner sanctum of ITN it was ruled that a freelance crew could not be allowed to accept such a prestigious award and it would be decided by four names going into a hat. The fact that our names were not included only brought home to me my old instructor's warning about the brickbats that may come your way. However, it seemed we did have an ally within ITN for just before the awards were announced, someone leaked the story to that feared columnist at the Daily Mail, Nigel Dempster, who made it clear that it had been filmed by a freelance crew and was causing some embarrassment to the Management.

We never knew if it was some kind of recompense, but not too long afterwards, we were given a spell on the 'Obits' programme. This was short for Obituary and was the department that kept all famous name's film interviews up to date. They ranged from politicians, sports men and women, TV personalities, authors, industrialists and top brass in the armed forces. The very nature of the department meant that all subjects were approaching a certain stage in life, although we never were able to find out at what age the interest in their health began.

The difficulty with these interviews was not giving any indication of the purpose of the film crew's visit, even more so when asked by the interviewee what programme it was for and when would it be transmitted. No known faces were used for the interview, the questions usually being asked by the producer using various ploys. Sometimes it was couched in the style of an in depth look at the life of someone who had passed on and had been known by the person being interviewed. Another guise was to prompt the person to make comparisons with their early life as opposed to what the present day state of affairs may have been. It was all very 'cloak and dagger' but always filmed in the pleasant surroundings of the subject's home. There were seven up-dates in all, namely, Eamonn Andrews, Sculptor, Henry Moore, Anna Neagle, Michael Redgrave, John Betjeman, Arthur Askey and the author, J.B.Priestley. He was most persistent in trying to find out the name of the programme, asking each of the crew in turn. This was followed up by his wife, the writer, Jacquetta Hawkes, who went round each of us to try and find out the name of the programme. 'JB' even followed us to the car while we were loading up the equipment to try and get some answers.

*

As we moved towards 1978 and 1979, we were reaching what has become known as the years of discontent. Industrial relations were at an all time low with major strikes in the car industry, and the fire service. Race relations were causing problems in towns where there was a large immigrant population. This in turn gave rise to large scale demonstrations by the National Front Movement. Striking council workers were causing havoc as rubbish piled up in the streets, even some funerals had to be postponed because grave diggers refused to cross picket lines. Prime Minister James Callaghan lost a great many votes when he arrived back from an overseas visit and answered a reporter's question about the crisis with the answer, "What crisis?"

We did an interview with Mrs Thatcher and Frank invited her to sign his book, showing her some of the famous names already listed. The comment she made became a great centre of interest for many years after. It read, 'Margaret Thatcher, Leader of the Conservative Party, hoping to become Britain's first woman Prime Minister.' Her hopes were answered in May, 1979.

So far it could be assumed that all television news stories were land based. But there were incidents which took place out at sea and if these were worthy of coverage, other than flying over in a helicopter or fixed wing aeroplane, then it would come within our brief. Although with hindsight I have a definite preference for land based stories! We had an early morning call to get to Yarmouth, just about as far east as you can go from Leicester. A Greek oil tanker had broken in two fifty kilometres off Lowestoft and was becoming a navigational hazard. The Navy were already out there and were planning to blow up the hull with several tons of explosives, so it would mean sailing out and transferring to the destroyer by means of a bosun's chair. All other shipping had been warned to stay clear of the safety zone. The sea was reasonably smooth on leaving Yarmouth, but by the time we were in sight of the Royal Navy, a heavy swell had developed, which was cheerfully estimated by the skipper of our ship as running at about three metres.

As we manoeuvred alongside with the chair in position, it was clear that the timing of the transfer had to be correct according to the rise and fall of each ship. This meant a great deal of trust had to be put in the sailors who would pull the chair at the right moment. It was an uneasy feeling sitting in a flimsy frame with the sea running at a fast speed below and around four metres' distance between each deck. Definitely not for the faint hearted. At a distance of one and a half kilometres, I had no idea how loud the bang would be. There was no chance of a take two and it certainly was not going to be the type of sound that you would have come across in film school. However, I had enough experience of bomb blasts so it was a mental calculation that worked. To give some indication of the force of the blast, when we arrived back at Yarmouth it had been heard by residents.

Another sea story involved the Royal Navy, but this time at the other side of England in the Irish Sea. We were called at eight p.m. to go to Fleetwood where a boat had been hired with the idea of going out to look for the Royal Navy search vessel that was trying to find a missing Tornado fighter. The wind was force seven and the skipper of the boat did not think much of our chances, but was prepared to try, only conceding defeat when we could barely make it to the harbour bar light. He then said it was becoming dangerous and we were certainly not going to argue with him. At four a.m. we knocked up the night porter at a sea front hotel and booked three rooms. When daylight came the wind was still blowing and on the advice of the boat owner, who thought the conditions would be worse further out to sea, we abandoned the idea and drove to Blackpool to spend the afternoon at the pleasure beach, including a ride on the Big Dipper!

Our reporter was Ken Rees, now on the staff at ITN but we had worked with him on a number of weekend stories when he was on detachment from HTV Bristol. He would in due course replace Martyn Lewis as the Northern Correspondent, which meant we would be seeing much more of him, including another sea story in the middle of the North Sea. Saturday was a better day with just a light wind and a calm sea, visibility was good and Skipper Gordon thought there was a good chance of finding the search vessel. Our boat was the MV Nayland, an ex pilot boat which had seen service along the Severn Estuary. It was well fitted out, including a very up to date galley that was well stocked. All we had to decide now was, who was going to be cook?

*

After four hours of sailing all we had seen was a Spanish trawler with huge beams for drawing in the nets. At a distance of fifteen kilometres we had been unsure if this was the search ship and had wasted considerable time in sailing to a distance where we could make a positive identification. The only other sizeable ships were the passenger ferries out of Heysham bound for Douglas or Dublin. It had been disappointing and we now needed to turn back towards Fleetwood as fuel was running low. The skipper turned on the radio to the normal 'shipping advice' channel and we heard a message being repeated warning all shipping to avoid a certain area, giving the necessary navigational information which he was able to plot on the chart. We were now convinced that this was the search area and we had been sailing too far north. Gordon did a quick calculation and reckoned we needed three hours sailing time to the map reference, adding he thought we should leave at five a.m.

It was five fifteen a.m. as we passed the harbour bar light and we were on a south westerly heading. The radio was still issuing the warning for all shipping to avoid the area that Gordon had plotted so it was just a matter of time. The conditions were perfect, very little wind, bright sunlight and a sea condition that looked like plastic sheeting. The contrast with two days earlier was hard to imagine. Just before eight a.m. we could make out a silhouette on the horizon which, with the help of a pair of binoculars Gordon had brought along, confirmed that it was a Royal Naval vessel. Gordon's navigation had been accurate, but when we were within perhaps four kilometres, his nerve let him down. He was convinced that we would now have been detected on their Radar and with the radio still transmitting a warning to all shipping to stay clear, he was beginning to doubt that we would be made welcome. From a news story point of view, this was what we had come for and unless they fired a shot across our bows, we convinced him to keep going. To quote Ken Rees, "All they can do is tell us to turn around and sail away. They are unlikely to clap us in irons."

So we kept going, right to within hailing distance when Ken announced who we were and the purpose of the voyage. To our amazement, their ship's tannoy replied with a, "Welcome aboard," as the crew began to lower boarding nets over the side. The ship was HMS 'Reclaim', a specially adapted minesweeper for deep water search and rescue. As we waited for lines to be attached, the Captain called down that we had arrived at an appropriate moment as the camera monitor was sending some very interesting pictures.

Moments later we were in the officer's quarters being served hot coffee and biscuits while introductions were made. The exciting news was that wreckage had been found and we were welcome to film the monitor screen, the Captain being of the opinion that it was an excellent way of showing the 'Top Brass' the purpose and effectiveness of his ship. The wreckage was lying at a depth of 100 metres and the images were of good and filmable quality. The only restriction imposed was not to film any views of the cockpit area as it had not yet been established whether or not the crew had been able to eject from the aircraft. It was remarkable footage and I knew that Ken would be already thinking about the evening news and how to get the film from the middle of the Irish Sea to the mainland. A Sea King helicopter was in the area helping with supplies, but the Captain, although smiling, did not think Ken's enquiry for a means of transporting him and the film to the mainland would go down well with Whitehall!

We cast off from HMS Reclaim at twelve noon. The sea was still calm and there was a breeze from the south west, but Gordon was concerned with the tide which would be ebbing as we neared the coast – he approximated our arrival around four p.m. The nearest regional ITV station was Granada in Manchester, but being Sunday they would have no film processing facility, which left the only alternative of catching a train to London Euston. The late evening news would be ten p.m., or possibly a little later if there was a film being shown. The plan was for Ken to leave immediately when we docked, and drive to Preston Station where he would leave the keys of his car at the ticket office, which we would collect, and I would drive his car to his home in Cheshire.

It all worked well and proved to be something of a scoop, for the BBC went on the air at nine p.m. saying that the search was continuing for a missing Tornado fighter, while News at Ten put out some remarkable pictures of the wreckage found in the Irish Sea. At the end of the bulletin the phone rang. It was Frank, we had received a 'herogram' from the Newsdesk. I was sipping a late night coffee, twelve hours earlier I had been doing the same in the middle of the Irish Sea. It was all quite surreal.

One story which passed unnoticed at the time but now quite poignant was one of the days we filled in for the ATV Newsdesk. We were assigned to a new and young reporter to cover a story in Matlock about custard tasting. It did not have much in the way of a news story but then this was regional television. But the young newcomer was Terry Lloyd who rapidly became a first class reporter, eventually joining ITN and whose life and career was to end so tragically in Iraq during the 2003 invasion

Another industrial story that had begun in the late seventies and spilled over into the new decade was the discord within British Steel. Steelworks were never the most glamorous places for film stories, so there was never much enthusiasm to travel to Sheffield, Scunthorpe, Corby or Bilston. Invariably, we would be interviewing trade union officials and it was around this time that we devised the 'union speak'. The more you heard it, the more irritating it became. We began to count the words in interviews; often I would hear Frank mutter the number under his breath. Some examples were, 'ongoing', 'confrontation', 'escalate', and the daddy of them all and highest points scorer in our idle game was, 'at this moment in time'. It became such a fixation amongst crews that one cameraman claimed he had heard a whole sentence made up from, "We do not want to escalate the ongoing confrontation at this moment in time." A copy of the recording would now be priceless!

I mentioned in earlier pages about the geographical knowledge or lack of, amongst assignment officers. In March, 1980, there was a tragedy in a Norwegian oilfield when a rig that was used as a floating hotel for workers overturned into stormy seas following the collapse of one of the five supporting legs. 123 workers died, but there were 89 survivors some of whom were flown to Britain. We had a six a.m. call to meet Ken Rees at Teeside Airport to try and film some of the injured men arriving and possibly obtain interviews, however, in the meantime pictures had been received of the sheared leg being towed towards Stavanger in Norway and the Newsdesk wanted coverage, either out at sea or the scene onshore around the harbour.

Frank and I had started the day thinking it would only be a short one and that we should be home for an evening meal. We had no change of clothes, no passports and probably around £10 each in cash. Now the brief was to get to Newcastle Airport, a light aeroplane had been hired to fly out to Stavanger where we would join an ocean-going tug and sail out to meet and film the remains of the supporting leg. It now meant a hasty dash into Darlington to find a camping shop that could kit us out with some all weather clothing and then to Newcastle to find an 8-seater Beechcraft belonging to Cabair all ready and waiting.

An aeroplane to yourself is quite an experience and Ken did the honours by waiting on us with coffee and nibbles. Sadly we were flying above the cloud base so there were no spectacular views to look down on, in fact the pilot advised us that for the last ten kilometres of the approach, he was flying 'blind'. We were under three hundred meters before we saw the runway dead ahead, which prompted Frank to sum up with, "Isn't Radar wonderful."

Being a private charter flight we came into a separate lounge away from the public area, perhaps it was assumed that we were V.I.Ps; for we were carrying the camera equipment as if ready for action and as the whole nation was in mourning for the disaster, just the mention that we were here to cover the Alexander Kielland story waived all formalities. What we did not think about at this stage was how we were going to leave the country without Passports or even attempt to re-enter Britain without them. But ITN had arranged for a hire car and booked a hotel so everything was organised in Norway except the weather. On the approach to the airport, the pilot had experienced strong crosswinds and down on the ground it was certainly a stiff breeze, not the type of weather you would want to be out at sea in. But we were putting out to sea in an ocean-going tug and surely they must be built to withstand any weather? How little we knew about the power of the sea!

Another staff crew and reporter had arrived from London and I am not sure how it was arrived at that we were the ones chosen for the sea voyage. At this span of years, I cannot recall any short straws being drawn or coins been tossed, nevertheless, around midnight we found ourselves at the dock and making our way onto the boat, which at first impression seemed to be all super structure with little towards the stern. Even tied to the quayside there was considerable movement so what was it going to be doing out at sea. The Captain was every inch a 'tugboat skipper' and welcomed us with, "Hello boys! Welcome aboard, it's force eight out there, are you good sailors?" We were soon going to find out!

Stavanger is situated on an estuary around 25 kilometres from the open sea so for the first two hours we were still within sight of land. The plan was to meet up with the salvage tug at first light, do all the filming required and then make a fast return to Stavanger to file a report. The skipper told us that we were sailing south west straight into the wind, adding jovially, that was the reason for the 'up and down'. It did little to help the way I was feeling and I could see Frank was not looking too good either. I was reminded of the old story about the Irish ferry from Holyhead, which went something like, 'for the first three hours you think it is going to sink and for the next three, you wish to hell it would'! Only Ken Rees seemed immune from the motion. Either he was a good sailor or he had taken a massive dose of some quelling potion.

Sickness was inevitable and we both made our way to the rear of the deck which was the lowest part of the ship and just tried to hang on to something The waves were so large that they were crashing over the bridge super structure and hitting us at the back of our necks as we leaned over the rail. We found a stairway leading down into the depths of the hold – it must have been the lowest part of the ship. Huge coils of rope provided some sort of sanctuary from the now receding sickness and a form of sleep took over.

Ken Rees had a zany sense of humour. The next thing I became aware of was being shaken roughly and a torch shone into my eyes from a few centimetres. A voice was telling me that the ship was sinking and we had to get into a lifeboat immediately. Then realisation struck as to who it was and where we were. I had to laugh. Frank had heard something and was now awake. It was

Ken's way of telling us that it was daylight and we were close to the salvage vessel.

Up on the bridge the skipper was offering coffee and Danish pastries and still in his jovial manner was telling us, "Better weather now boys, only force six." We declined his offer of breakfast and could not see much difference in the size of the waves. The sheared leg of the rig seemed to be larger than the salvage ship and made an eerie sight as it rose and fell with the motion of the waves. The distance was about 100 metres and we were able to cover most angles, then Ken suggested he did a piece to camera. Now it was our turn to get the jokes in. "Stand a little closer to the rail Ken. No, back a bit more. No, a bit more, try standing on the rail that should do it." As the skipper turned for base, he told us he was turning on full power and the ship took on a steadier feel. I could see what he meant about the waves being smaller, now there were fewer which washed over the roof of the bridge. When we finally docked in Stavanger and bid our farewells, the skipper said he had an hour's drive to his home and a warm bed. The dock was full of cars and we were curious to know what the skipper of an ocean-going tug would drive to go with his macho image. We roared with laughter when he got into a Morris Marina and as he drove out of the dock, true to form, there was a little piece of body trim hanging down. We all felt much better.

There was only one flight a day to London, which we had now missed, but we were saved because we could put the film on an afternoon flight to Aberdeen and have Grampian Television collect and process the film before transmitting it to London. ITN could then edit a package and include Ken's piece to camera. It made both the early evening bulletin and News at Ten. During dinner at the hotel a message from London came through which read, 'Congrats to those who were all at sea.'

In the short time I spent in Norway I found it a delightful country with charming people who had such a nice genial attitude to life, to say nothing of their excellent command of English in hotels and shops. I always had a mind to return one day for a holiday but I think work had a habit of getting in the way. We did, however, manage a little sightseeing in the few hours we had before catching the once a day flight to London. Going through the duty free shop, Frank decided on taking three bottles of Scotch whisky back. I think he was only allowed two, but I had offered to carry one as part of my allowance. We now came to the problem of no Passports. We were still carrying the film equipment without any flight cases and with the help of Ken Rees, who was able to show his Passport and vouch for us, the Norwegian Customs man must have been of the opinion that someone had authorised our entry and now we were leaving his country. Ken was staying behind so if there was any 'comeback' at least they had a suspect to round up. The fun was to begin when we landed at Heathrow. It was to cost Frank three bottles of whisky!

There were very few passengers on the flight; most of them were Norwegian which meant they would exit through a separate channel. We came to the one marked 'UK Citizens' and as there appeared to be no one checking documents, except for an officer sitting in a small cabin, we kept going.

We had only gone perhaps three metres when this official voice roared out, "Oi, you two."

I jokingly said, "Shall we make a run for it?" but returned to him and said, "You are not going to believe this but three days

179

ago we flew out of Newcastle in a private plane without our Passports and have been covering the Norwegian oil rig disaster off Stavanger."

"What identification do you have then?" he asked scathingly. I pulled out my Scotland Yard Press Pass and pointed to the serial number and told him that would identify me and the job I was assigned to .He seemed mildly convinced. Then he turned to Frank and said, "Do you have one as well?" Frank had the camera strap over one shoulder, a camera battery and charger over the other and his bag of duty free goodies. As he reached into his inner pocket he had to try and steady the straps from slipping off and that was when it happened. The handle of the plastic carrier bag broke and fell at the officer's feet flooding the floor of his cabin with the contents of three bottles of best Scotch whisky. The fumes were almost over powering. We suggested he got out quick before becoming intoxicated. We had around twenty minutes to make a connecting flight to Newcastle.

It was March 31st – in fact by the time I arrived home it was one thirty a.m. on April 1st. At ten a.m. the phone was ringing. Could we get to Sleaford in Lincolnshire where there was a reported outbreak of Meningitis. We spent the next three days there. Some of the hospital ward scenes were quite harrowing and in complete contrast to the previous story providing another example of the crazy business I was in. At the weekend we were in Nottingham filming two young skaters called Jane Torvill and Christopher Dean who were making quite a name for themselves and were tipped to go on to greater things!

A story in the last few days of 1980 marked the end of an era it being the last time we worked with Martyn Lewis. He was now a regular news reader at ITN and the story we were doing was probably intended for the 'And Finally' slot. It was about a team of Karate experts who had made a wager that they could demolish a house faster than a bulldozer. We had done many stories with him and covered a great many miles. He was renowned for the distances covered to bring a story to the screen, so much so that one of the staff crews made up a trophy comprising a shield and a speedometer and called it 'The Mileage Award'. Martyn was always attributed with creating the 'piece to camera' and for certainly inserting it in the middle of a story thus preventing a sub editor removing it if he was short on programme time.

1981 could be called the year of the Yorkshire Ripper. Not the nicest of titles for sure but covered in depth from a news angle, if only because of the many false clues that were pursued and the missed opportunities through lack of co-ordination. We had an invite to film inside the main centre and to see the rows of filing cabinets and filing systems in use. It would have taken a staff of several hundred to keep it up to date.

The most gruesome task was interviewing members of the family of victims, sometimes more than once in cases where they had firstly gone missing then turned up as another body. Again at the other extreme, a story that brought crowds out onto the streets with placards protesting the decision was the sacking of Meg Richardson. Who? I hear you chorus. This was the name of the character played by Noele Gordon since 1964 in the ATV soap, 'Crossroads'. Frank, in fact had filmed the first scenes on location in 1964 before they had built studio sets. Miss Gordon was not giving any interviews, but condescended to an ITN interview when she saw who the cameraman was. It pleased the reporter Tim Ewart, who had only recently joined ITN.

There were more changes on the way. This time of a technical nature. There had been tremendous advances in portable video equipment and now it was becoming accepted in broadcast circles which sounded the death knell of the film camera, along with the problems of processing and lighting. It was by no means making the sound recordist's job any easier, as the first separate recorders introduced by Sony were probably three times heavier than what they had been carrying. But film still had a little life left. With an easing of the 'Cold War', the Ministry of Defence allowed a press open day at the famous 'Golf Ball 'tracking station on the North Yorkshire Moors at Fylingdale. We were allowed inside the golf balls with the dire warning not to step in front of the scanner. The MOD official put it another way, "You will be very crispy bacon in no time." Also there were a crew from Tyne Tees using the new portable video system, already dubbed ENG; or Electronic News Gathering. When they finished and returned to their edit truck, it was discovered that everything they had shot had been erased. Whereas film remained untouched and our pictures went out on News at Ten.

One last hurrah for film on major news events was the opening of the Humber Bridge. Work had started in 1973 and it was planned to be a toll bridge. On the opening day in June, 1981 there were long queues of vehicles all celebrating the 'first' something. Cars had signs in the windscreen declaring it was the first Lada to cross, or maybe the first Reliant 3-wheeler. Someone had a lawnmower on a trailer claiming that was a first. Frank joined in the fun by putting a sign on the camera car saying he was wearing the first blue underpants to cross. But as always there were losers, in this case it was the old ferry that had been running since 1826. It closed the same day but not before it had one last fling of publicity on News at Ten.

We received a call from ITN to be at the Market Place in Nottingham for a certain time. A taxi was due to arrive from London containing a complete ENG kit which we were to take over and use until the end of the year. Frank asked if there was a manual included and was told a staff recordist would give us some tuition. When Harold arrived he had a few notes scribbled on the back of an old envelope and any tuition consisted of 'that lead goes in there, that's where you switch on, that is where the battery fits'. And with that he was back in the taxi on his way back south. We had met up with John Toker who was on detachment from Granada Television. Before long we had been briefed to cover a story in Nottingham where there had been a robbery and a murder and that was our introduction to the new technology.

For the next five days we roamed the north with stories in Bradford, Liverpool, Preston and Manchester. We had proved the 'Doubting Thomas's' were wrong when everyone had said to handle the new video equipment you had to attend a two week course, learn new techniques, adapt to the new format. We took to it like the proverbial 'ducks'.

One story covered was the closing of the final Belle Vue Circus in Manchester where we really got into the spirit of circus life by following the Ring Master down the tunnel to the strains of 'Entry of the Gladiators'. Bursting through the curtain as all spotlights were turned on came the ebullient Norman Long accompanied by an ITN crew. After the show was over and we were enjoying the buffet, I fed Frank a story that I knew the performers would enjoy. He started with, "My soundman used to be in the circus and he was very popular. He was the only one who could get the tent back in the bag." Frank got all the laughs, but then I always figured myself as the 'straight man'. We met the lion tamer, Martin Lacy, billed as, 'The man that fear forgot'. Ken Rees wanted to film him putting his head in the lion's mouth but as he was asking a fee of £1000 dropped the idea. Martin did, though, let us in on how it was done without the lion being able to close its mouth. He swore us all to secrecy not to reveal it!

About this time a series of 'Material' jokes were doing the rounds which became de rigueur for film crews. They usually centred around someone who had just bought a new coat or jacket, to which the uninterested onlooker would reply along the lines of, "What a pity they didn't have your size." Or, "It's nice material, you should have a jacket made out of it." They became the type of answer to be used almost without thinking. Which was how I came to cross swords with Sophia Loren in the Holiday Inn, Birmingham. She was over in Britain promoting her new book about Italian cooking and was doing the usual rounds of book shop signings, radio and television interviews and all the press pages. She had a suite of rooms which were being used for all the press and TV coverage and we were to follow the BBC crew with our interview.

As I leant over to clip a Sony personal microphone to the lapel of her dress, her dark eyes flashed and she hissed, "Be careful, sis cost 800 Francs in Paree."

Without thinking I just replied, "It will look nice when it's finished." The press corps laughed but she didn't understand the joke and was possibly about to explode into some Latin expletives when she realised that the purpose of it all was to sell her book.

She just turned on that magic smile and said, "Oh you press people are all the same."

But there was also more serious news. Argentine troops had invaded the Falkland Islands and Mrs Thatcher was carrying out her threat to send a task force.

We spent two days covering the preparations of Vulcan bombers and Harrier jump jet fighters at RAF Waddington and RAF Wittering, plus interviews with crews and Defence Ministers. All the answers had to be vetted by an MOD 'minder' and no caption names of air crew could be used. With or without names, they all looked very young for the job they were about to embark on. Not unlike the boys of forty years earlier who had faced a similar task. However, as history shows, they did a superb job in a war zone that was 7000 miles from home.

We also covered the land forces on manoeuvres in the Black Mountains of Carmarthenshire, where live mortars and howitzers were being used. To be able to film them in realistic surroundings, we had to agree to join one of the platoons and to take orders, much to the delight of a veteran Sergeant Major who treated us like raw recruits under fire for the first time. As if the live barrage was not enough, a formation of rocket firing Tornados flew over and demolished a row of mock houses.

Frank and I had now worked together for eight years, during which time we had turned in some big headlining stories. But alongside the film work, my record company had been growing to proportions which now needed more time devoting to the catalogue which in reality meant more time spent behind a desk. We came to an understanding that I would take a year out on a form of sabbatical break and as there was a recordist available in the midlands area, this would still enable me to be available without the need for round the clock duty.

BBC Midlands based at Pebble Mill became aware of my availability and used me for holiday or sickness cover along with a general range of local stories on days which I was able to choose. Some of the stories, however, were hardly in the top flight of news worthiness. My work diary reminds me of; The Flying Granny. Goats Milk Production and Britain's largest collection of Dinky Toys. When the year came to an end there was a trace of impatience to be back under the ITN banner.

In my absence, there had been a change of Northern Reporter. This was now Michael McMillan from Northern Ireland. By coincidence, I had known his father, Dick McMillan, who was a cameraman in Belfast and had covered many stories during the troubled period of the 'seventies'. A Northern Office had now been established at the Midland Hotel in Manchester, including a full edit suite and a mobile unit manned by two editors on a rota basis. Such was the difference now with the advancement of ENG. We were no longer known as the Midlands Crew. We just turned up wherever we were sent.

Many of the stories were with Michael McMillan (or 'Mickmack' as the London crews had dubbed him!), but we still met up with London reporters and I note from my diary that a number were with Terry Lloyd, now a very competent and likeable part of the ITN operation. He had a most charming and persuasive manner, as was once shown when we were trying to interview the daughter of Ruth Ellis, who was the last woman to be hanged in Britain. She at first refused flatly to be filmed, or even a voice only recording, but Terry gently coaxed her by explaining how it could help her campaign in showing that her Mother was not the harridan that many of the national newspapers were portraying.

I have already mentioned my liking for 'epitaphs'. One of them could read, "I was arrested by Christopher Dean." Yes, the same Christopher Dean of Torvill and Dean fame. We had got to know both of them well following their continued success and it just so happened that Chris was a serving police constable in Nottingham attached to the Court House and Town Hall. We had arrived at the Town Hall to record an interview with the leader of the local Tory party.

However, when the controlling Labour group found out, we were ordered to leave.

As we were waiting for our reporter to arrive from London, we refused to move until he had briefed us. Again we were threatened that unless we left immediately, the police would be called and forcibly remove us. We decided to call his bluff and told him to go ahead, upon which, he turned and headed off downstairs. Ten minutes later he was back with a police constable, which of course turned out to be Chris Dean, who, upon seeing both of us greeted us with our first names and went into a comical routine along the lines of, "Hello, Hello, Hello, what's going on here then?"

The Labour councillor was completely bewildered and as our reporter and the local Tory leader had now arrived and explained that the interview was to be filmed in the Councillor's private room, he was now reduced to listening to Chris explain that it was not a police matter and he did not have the authority to refuse admittance to the opposition party guests. As we were leaving the Town Hall, he was still hovering around the entrance and I suggested to our reporter that I asked how did the humble pie taste? As he was the then Political Correspondent at ITN, he suggested that it was, "Gilding the lily a little too much." And he was right.

Life always seemed to be in the fast lane and so it proved when we had a job to do at Silverstone Race Track. Jaguar were planning an all out assault on winning at Le Mans and had a prototype ready for testing. When the car was wheeled out, there seemed to be barely room for the driver let alone a cameraman and recordist, but as this was just a prototype test shell we managed to fit in somewhere. Frank was wedged next to the driver, while I was lying under the cross struts and anti-roll bars. I was virtually on my back with no vision other than being able to adjust the record level. Having no vision to judge speed, I could only assume it was fast by the way I sensed the car sliding through corners. I did have sight of one dial on the panel which was frequently reading 1000 and sometimes higher. I had no idea how many laps we completed but felt no sense of disappointment when I heard the exhaust note fall to a bearable level and forward motion began to reduce. When we had finally extricated ourselves and were trying to look unconcerned, I asked the test driver about the meaning of the dial reading around the 1000 figure.

"It tells me my speed," was his reply.

Still trying to appear unconcerned, I nonchalantly said, "What ninety-five or a hundred?"

Giving me a, 'let's humour him' look. He said, "Well it's multiplied by ten so that makes it pushing a hundred and thirty mph." As test driving racing cars was his living, I thought it best not to make any further comment. Both Frank and I used to get a little irritated when a member of the public came up and said, "I bet you've got an interesting job."

Before we leave this period, just two more silly stories that may give an idea of the everyday life of a news crew on location. We were driving through Lincolnshire on our way to an ex RAF bomber station, where the hangars had been converted into grain stores. Our reporter was Keith Hatfield who had been with ITN since 1967, even before 'News at Ten' was launched, and despite some life threatening moments in his career, he had always managed to stay on the plus side of sanity, save for an occasional lapse into a bizarre type of humour. His personality and charm were unbelievable when it came to persuasion as was the case on this warm summer's day.

I was sitting in the rear of the camera car with the window down enjoying the cooling airstream, when Frank, a persistent smoker, flicked the ash from his cigarette out of the driver's window. It came straight back in and hit my tie smack in the middle, burning a perfectly symmetrical hole, the nylon material taking on a glazed charred appearance. We arrived in the village and noted that the local inn had a food sign displayed, so we pulled into the car park. The lady behind the bar said we were too late for any food and that the chef had already gone. Then Keith turned on the charm, first explaining we had driven from London. No she was sorry but there was nothing she could do. Then he tried by telling her we were returning to the RAF base. She still apologised that there was no food. Then he came out with the most brilliant impromptu pretence. He asked her if she had noted my tie, adding that the round burn was a symbol that very few men could wear as it indicated they had survived excruciating hardship in returning to their home base, which was the reason why they had clubbed together to bring me back on this day which was the anniversary of my ordeal. Fifteen minutes later we were enjoying scrambled egg, bacon, beans, toast and to finish, a slice of Black Forest gateau and cream.

There are a number of reasons to remember the next tale. It was New Year's Day, 1981, and we had been called to Haseley Manor, in Warwickshire, a huge old house set in a few hundred acres of park land. It was owned by British Leyland, being used for conferences and some research projects. It had been acquired in the more affluent days of the company and would soon disappear under Government restructuring of the whole of this troublesome arm of the Midlands car industry. For weeks there had been strikes and stoppages over pay and labour relations, now there was to be one final meeting. Both sides had been given ultimatums to reach a settlement so we knew we would be in for a long wait. A room had been set aside for press use which was well furnished with comfortable chairs and plenty of table space for typewriters and reporters' paperwork. It was also well supplied from the kitchens with tea, coffee and sandwiches. ITN had sent along Alistair Stewart on one of his first big assignments, but I doubt even he knew what a marathon it was to become.

The call time was ten a.m. and being a Bank Holiday, most technicians would be starting their day at a 'times two' rate. To be still there at seven p.m. was still not out of the ordinary, as it was not unusual for talks between management and unions to drag on into the evening. By the time ten p.m. came round and we were totting up twelve hours, calculators were out working the amount so far. At midnight, a break was called and both sides came out to make a statement. It seemed one problem was how much the Government stake was going to be, to which one journalistic wag replied, come and see some of the crews here, they should be able to bale you out! Another hour passed and another break was called. Still no definite settlement figure, except on the calculators! Finally at two thirty a.m. both sides emerged with smiling faces and everyone was scrambling for interviews. Neither side would say they had lost. Management claimed to have got a satisfactory result. But then so did the union leader. There were winners of course, those with a calculator in their pocket. The next three days were spent covering the factories, the workers and their families, both sides in the dispute, even local business and shops. My diary shows that four days were charged as ten days!

*

"It's all George Orwell's fault." This was the catch phrase to make light of any doom and gloom which occurred after the start of 1984. There were pundits who said it was only a matter of time before there was a major confrontation between Government and the Trade Union movement along the lines of the General Strike of 1926. This was certainly indicated during the first week of the New Year which began in Birkenhead with a strike by dockers. The next day we were down at Stoke on Trent to film miners who were holding an underground 'sit in' protest, while others had picketed the entrance to prevent lorries entering or leaving. We were back the next day when all production at the pit stopped and an all out strike was declared. Little did we think of what this action would lead to and how it would change many lives. But this was still only January.

February was filled with industrial stories, many of them connected with miners who were being balloted on taking strike action. The main protagonist was Arthur Scargill, leader of the Yorkshire miners and President of the National Union of

Mineworkers since 1982. Arthur became the villain of the piece in many eyes with his rampaging on television about those running the National Coal Board and even the country. And he never made any secret about his hatred of the Thatcher Government. Frank and I were to spend a lot of time in his company, in his office at Sheffield, on picket lines and even at his house. If you could wean him off politics for a brief spell, he was an interesting person with a deep knowledge of current affairs. He was also a big movie buff with a liking for the films of Burt Lancaster, one of his favourites being 'Elmer Gantry'.

When the Head of the Coal Board announced that they were planning to axe 20,000 jobs and close 20 pits on economic grounds, they were laying the touch paper for strike action throughout the British coalfield. The fuse was lit at Cortonwood colliery near Barnsley when workers were told that their pit was to close in five weeks. The Yorkshire NUM set in motion the strike which, with the support of the Scottish NUM and it was hoped all other regions, would bring a halt to the nation's industry. They soon had the backing of miners from Durham, Kent and South Wales.

For the next eleven days we covered the area from Northumberland to South Wales, taking in the coal regions of Durham, Lancashire, Yorkshire, Nottinghamshire and Leicestershire on the way. In the eleven day period, we stayed at nine different hotels. To begin with the Newsdesks at ITN and the BBC were wrong footed as to the seriousness of the strike, leaving the two of us to virtually carry the story for the first week. On the reporting side we had Patrick Bishop, Ken Rees and, new boy at Channel 4 News, Edward Sturton, who caused something of a stir up the Rhondda Valley at five a.m. by trying to interview pickets dressed in a Crombie overcoat with an astrakhan collar and a rolled copy of the Daily Telegraph under his arm!

ITN had now realised the strike was not a localised story confined to a couple of mining areas and began planning maximum coverage. Their policy would be for the regional stations to cover day to day picket lines, plus other attempts to blockade coal deliveries, while we, along with three London crews, would be available to cover any outbreaks of violence. When we registered at the Royal Hotel in Nottingham, little did we know we were to be there for the next six weeks!

Using Nottingham as a base meant we could cover the whole of the Nottinghamshire coalfield and have quick access to any trouble in Leicestershire or Staffordshire as Mr Scargill began to step up his 'flying pickets'. Nottinghamshire miners had long benefited from a production agreement because their seams were easier to work and output per pit was higher than many areas. They were, therefore, not immediately in full agreement with the Yorkshire NUM which is why the nightly convoys of cars came south from Yorkshire as a means of persuasion. We were very soon to get into a nightly ritual to cover all this activity. It began with a three a.m. alarm call, then a meeting in the hotel lobby between a news editor and reporters to decide which pits to visit, then away from the hotel by three thirty a.m. We would usually arrive back at the hotel around eight a.m. for breakfast, with perhaps a couple of hours to freshen up. Then it was out again to film any material for News at One and the early evening news. At this point we would possibly be too far distant from the hotel, so any break time was a matter of luck. Then it would be off again to cover for News at Ten, using 'links vehicle' to transmit unedited packages direct to London. If all went well we would hope to reach the hotel by ten thirty p.m. with all the jibes still running around your head.

"Aye up. It's 'Lies at Ten'. Put that leet aart."

"ITV, Independent Tory Views."

"Why don't you get a proper job?"

"ITN Idiot Thatcher News."

On a good night you could have up to four hours' sleep!

As we came down each morning I began to liken it to how wartime bomber crews must have felt at their pre-raid briefings. Some targets were known for heavy flak and night fighters, while others would be less dangerous. Some of the pits were gaining reputations for trouble where we would be treated as the invaders. Dodging missiles became the norm as the strike intensified and we quickly realised that it was necessary to park the camera car up to a mile from the pit entrance if we wanted to find it in a drivable state. The galling thing about the whole affair was, as the strike extended into months, several trade unions began contributing to the NUM hardship funds with the film technicians union being one of the largest donors. Trying to explain this to strikers as they hurled abuse or missiles, or even just spat at you, was lost in the heated moment.

As the violence increased, large numbers of police from other county forces were drafted in and the Newsdesk was interested to see where and how they were being accommodated. Many police stations were providing sleeping facilities, but we had noted a convoy of mini buses driving down a track into woods near Ollerton in Nottinghamshire and local knowledge provided the answer that there was a disused army camp in the woods. We planned our own commando style raid headed by reporter Ken Rees and entered the woods where we came upon the typical army style wooden huts where men were relaxing, or doing simple washing chores. Some were kicking a ball in a five-a-side contest. Nobody challenged us as we went about filming the setting, everyone assuming that we were there with full permission of somebody and the ITN sticker on the camera gave some credibility. Ken even' threw a couple of questions at one group and we soon had a mini 'vox pop' sequence about their feelings of leaving the relatively rural settings of Sussex or Kent to come to this wild and untamed industrial setting.

*

All was going well until a sergeant came up and asked who had authorised the visit and given clearance to speak to off duty police officers. It was time to 'own up', which Ken did in a most condescending manner, but it was not enough. We were told to "Wait right there," while higher authority was contacted. Discretion became the better part of valour and we decided to walk, very quickly, away. The fast walking became a run when a voice bellowed, "Stop those men." Despite our best efforts of avoiding entanglement in brambles, long unkempt grass and low hanging branches, to say nothing of the weight and encumbrance of the equipment, we were overtaken and apprehended. I did, however, have time to eject the cassette.

After we made a confession that we were just after a story, the first thing the inspector asked for was the video cassette. Without protesting, I took out a cassette from the recorder case and passed it to him, ignoring protests from Ken that he had no authority to seize ITN property. A sergeant and three burly officers then escorted us the rest of the way to the boundary fence and left us with the parting shot, "Get your posteriors over that fence fast and don't come back." Or words to that effect! Back at the camera car Ken was still going on about how I should have stood my ground and not given him the tape, when I pulled out of my jacket the original cassette and handed it to him. All six foot six of him grabbed my shoulders and he planted a sloppy kiss on my forehead.

Frank, never one to openly dish out praise, drew heavily on a cigarette and just said, "Ah! Well done Batman." It was a story that gained a lot of mileage around bars across the midlands.

The mayhem went on night after night. The worst pits were those where some men were trying to defy the strike and continuing working, this was where the greatest dangers from thrown objects came. Anything that came easily to hand would be thrown from the back of the crowd. It was even worse at night with just illumination from the lighting man's battery lamp, known colloquially as a 'hand basher'. We had to be wary of surging crowds too. Frank and I were connected by a cable between the camera and recorder and if either was to stumble the chances of regaining your feet were very limited. Where possible, we relied on the police presence for our safety, but when they responded to a surge 'en masse', the place to be was definitely not in the middle.

By the end of six weeks, someone must have noted that we, outwardly at least, had taken on a Zombie like nature, which in view of the lack of sleep and regular nourishment was hardly surprising. We were rather inelegantly looked upon as being 'pit happy' and in need of a change. In late April we were taken off the miners' strike to cover what some would consider, more conventional stories that kept to regular hours and meal breaks. These included coverage of the Teacher's conference in

Blackpool, a local by-election, a story on modern Shakespeare at a Liverpool Theatre and with the forthcoming fortieth anniversary of the D-Day Landings, a chance to meet and interview some survivors. As two old ex servicemen, this was a story that both Frank and I enjoyed working on. After listening to some of the stories of survival, despite severe injuries endured for hours before being rescued, it made any trouble that an industrial dispute could create pale into insignificance.

The break ended all too quickly and in no time we were back on the 'old routine'. At the first conflict Frank was heard to say, "It seems like we haven't been away." The situation had worsened in so far as crowds. There were now strikers from other areas joining the 'flying pickets' and, inevitably, others were using the occasion for their own ends with a chance to attack the forces of law and order. ITN increased their coverage with additional crews and we were now joined by Colin Baker. The very same Colin Baker of the famous 'piece to camera' that has become immortalised on the programme, 'It'll be Alright on the Night'. For those not yet 'au fait' with it the gist of the sign off goes, "Colin Baker, Thames News. Cold. Wet, Very Wet. Wife, Kids, Dog, Pxxxxx off, thoroughly Pxxxxx off."

At least he was recognised on the picket lines and it gave them something different to shout when we arrived. As for Mr Scargill, he was still predicting that coal stocks at power stations were dwindling and the country would soon be plunged into darkness with power cuts. He kept maintaining the stockpiles that were visable at the power stations were only subterfuge with nothing in the middle, like huge 'doughnuts'. We took to the air with a one man helicopter company and proved his theory wrong. The coal trains were still running. Our pilot was an Indian who had flown with the Indian Air Force and had come to Britain to start up his own 'Heli-Hire' company. Being hired by a national television channel was a big boost to his 'client list' and he was keen to co-operate with any shots we wanted. The Newsdesk had insisted that we show the height of the coal stocks, along with proof that the rails entering the power station were shiny and in regular use. Frank asked for a low shot of the stockpiles, with a zooming in effect by the helicopter as it slowly approached. We were no more than three metres from the ground and moving forward, when to my horror, I realised we were passing a steel electricity pylon! We were flying under 132,000 volts of National Grid power! Frank got his shot, totally oblivious to how it was achieved. What he didn't see in the viewfinder was of no importance. Now we wanted an airborne tracking shot showing the rails and again the pilot was only too happy to oblige.

But by now, someone on the ground had become aware of us and had sent out a Land Rover to investigate. The pilot saw it, realised that he could be in breach of some law if his aviation number was noted and began to increase speed. With so many overhead cables, it was impossible to rise and it turned into a chase sequence reminiscent of a James Bond film, as we dodged around buildings before being able to gain height. If we were leaving the 'frying pan', we were entering the 'fire'. The pilot was unfamiliar with the radio call channel for East Midlands Airport, into whose airspace we were about to enter. As he tried each channel in turn with no response, a flare was fired from the control tower to draw his attention to the danger followed by another. At last he found the channel and a very irate controller told him to alter course and reduce height to 100 metres and adopt a hover position. We remained like this for several minutes and my thoughts were with Frank, as it was almost twenty years ago since he had plummeted from a similar altitude when the engine failed over forests in Wales. He seemed unconcerned though and like me was relieved when we saw a British Midland in-bound flight from Dublin touch down safely. We had been heading across the flight path!

We did several more aerial reconnaissance flights over power stations and railway coal yards, however, following our report, ITN used a different helicopter hire company. Mr Scargill's threats of power cuts and blackouts were diminishing as March and April proved to be the mildest for many years and the demand for electricity was well within the generator's capacity, even if coal supplies were erratic. The railway unions were not giving their full support to the miners and with more workers returning to their pits, Nottinghamshire was becoming a lost cause. Even the 'flying pickets' were finding motoring costs prohibitive with no wages coming in. It was time for a change in their strike policy. However, before this happened, there was another break in our routine, although not in pleasant circumstances.

We had just arrived back at the hotel around ten p.m. after the usual night patrol and were about to sit down for the last serving of dinner, when a call came over the hotel speaker asking for someone from ITN to contact their office. Frank came back to the table and said, "Forget the meal we have to get to Abbeystead." He handed me the note with vague directions, which said, 'Take M6 north to Lancaster. It's on the right!' This was quite detailed compared to some directions from the assignment's desk. I recall we were once sent to look for a crashed aircraft near a railway viaduct in North Wales! Little did we know that this was the end of our stay at the Royal Hotel, Nottingham. The centre of the strike action was about to move to Sheffield.

There had been an explosion in a water pumping station, caused by a spark igniting Methane gas. At the time there was a group of local villagers being shown around and nine of them had died in the huge blast. By the time we arrived at the scene it was three a.m. the next day, which meant it was twenty-four hours since we had slept. There was little to be seen immediately and it was only when daylight came that the full extent of the damage became apparent. The underground chamber where the visiting party had been was totally destroyed with massive concrete roof supports just tossed aside like matchwood.

It was a day of disaster and tragedy and one which dragged on into the early evening. When we finally arrived at the hotel and booked in for an early night, my work diary shows it was 43 hours since I had last been to bed. The following day was much the same, with interviews around the village where all the people had come from. So often did we see a sleepy village that was suddenly taken over by media people and pushed into the nation's spotlight. For the next few days, the name of St. Michael's on Wyre was leading all bulletins and fronting the daily papers, until that is, another major story came along to replace it. This time the name was Orgreave.

As we drove back south we knew there was a strong possibility of being called for a midland's story as we were already on the road. Sure enough it came as we were leaving the M6 motorway, only fifty miles from home. Midlands Trade Unionists had planned a rally at Cannock and two local MPs were due to speak, by coincidence, we were only fifteen miles away. The area around Cannock had a long mining tradition and it was the current strike that was high on the agenda. Miners were being urged to join a contingent that was planning to support the Yorkshire miners who were to now concentrate their numbers around their own pits. Mr Scargill now had a new plan. At the beginning of the strike, the NUM had agreed that some movement of coal could be permitted for the production of coke. This was used in the steel furnaces at British Steel plants and was needed to prevent damage to the blast furnaces, but it was claimed by the Miners' leader, that the agreed amount was being exceeded. The plan was now to picket the coke works at Orgreave on the outskirts of Sheffield and prevent deliveries to the Steel works at Scunthorpe. We were called out late on May 28 to travel to the site in preparation for what was believed to be the largest gathering so far. And so it proved to be. We were now to take up residence at the Grosvenor Hotel, Sheffield for the next nine weeks.

The first day of the 'Battle of Orgreave' began in the early hours as police tried to break up groups of pickets...Their intention was to try and stop the convoy of lorries that were due to arrive to collect coke for the steel works at Scunthorpe. Failing that they would make an all out push to prevent them leaving as they were expecting more support later in the day. The greatest danger was from stones and other missiles which were being thrown aimlessly at the police lines. To counteract this, they now deployed new tactics with squads of officers in full riot gear who were able to seize likely ringleaders from the front of the crowd. I and Russ, the lighting man, could hopefully keep a look out for any danger of stones coming our way as Frank, was in effect, divorced from what was going on around him by looking at the events through the viewfinder. The lorries arrived and were able to enter the coking plant and were not expected to leave for at least two hours, which gave the police time to bring in more reinforcements. At all costs the lorries had to move away together, any delay or stoppage would be fatal should the picket lines surge forward with force and get amongst the convoy and as they held the slightly higher ground, there was a chance of this happening. When the time came for the gates to open the police with long shields moved into action and charged the nearest crowd. This had the effect of scaring and scattering them into confusion which allowed the lorries to start moving at high speed towards the motorway. Out on the M18 police cars ensured that no traffic overtook the convoy during the journey back to Scunthorpe, but one danger that was to manifest itself in the coming days was from the overbridges where pickets tried to hurl slabs of concrete down onto the lorries.

Day one had been violent, but the worst was yet to come. It was clear that if we were to keep in touch with all the action and the other crews and reporters, we needed some form of communication. The only means of coverage with two-way radios was to have the transmitter on some high point that could give a range of around two miles. A local communications company was contacted and they installed the transmitter on the roof of a high block of flats which was perfect for the location of the coke works. It also gave ITN a tremendous advantage over other channels in being able to be in the right place. It also became a 'nice little earner' for the communications company, as it was forgotten about when the Orgreave trouble subsided and remained in place for a further three months. Nobody in the accountants department queried the monthly arrival of the invoices and just kept signing the cheques! Day two began with violence long before the lorries were due to arrive. Mr Scargill was an early riser too and was on the picket lines in support of his members who found new motivation from his presence. It was estimated that there were over 6000 pickets that confronted the police riot force, using dogs and mounted police who began to move forward, driving the strikers further up the lane away from the gates of the coke works. But sheer weight of numbers meant that retaliation would bring a charge which the police would find difficult to withstand and so the horses were deployed in the first of a number of charges, along with the 'snatch squads' who arrested around one hundred miners, including Mr Scargill. He appeared at Rotherham Magistrates' Court that afternoon and we managed to snatch an interview with him as he was leaving. It was the occasion when he delivered the quote, "There have been scenes of almost unbelievable brutality, reminiscent of a Latin American police state." The last days of May and the first week of June saw some of the worst violence, only kept in check with repeated charges by mounted police and the foot squads. Missile throwing was now organised in waves on a command from someone in the crowd, doubling the danger of being hit. Despite the summer heat, we had taken to wearing full winter anoraks packed with spare tape boxes and camera batteries which if you had enough warning of incoming missiles at least you could turn and take the brunt of the attack.

Some pickets had taken to throwing less savoury objects such as plastic bags filled with thinners or paint stripper or at worst urine. Obviously the velocity of these was not far and they were usually spotted by the snatch squads, nevertheless, it was yet another hazard to be avoided. As each day passed, they still had not achieved their object of halting the convoy and it was becoming obvious that the numbers of strikers was getting smaller. However, the police numbers remained constant with reserves never far away parked in lines of unmarked vans, but the situation was still volatile and there was to be one last battle.

Trouble began on a Sunday afternoon when police had tried to make an arrest in Maltby, near Rotherham. There was a large mine here which we had visited on a number of occasions, but support for the strike was solid. What started as a simple police operation, soon turned into a full-scale riot with the police outnumbered. We found ourselves trapped in the main street with rioters at both ends and although we may not have been the object of their resentment, neither of us fancied the idea of plea bargaining or even trying to explain we were from Channel 4. Over the last four weeks, that channel had been putting out a number of programmes in support of the miner's claim and it had found favour several times to let it be known you were working for them. We edged our way into a small front garden thinking there may have been a passage between the houses but there was no way out. Then the door was opened by a pensioner who sensed the danger and guided us through to his back door, telling us he was a retired miner and totally disagreed with all the violence. We just had time to say how much we agreed with him and apologised for disturbing the pigeons before we clambered over the wall. As we were leaving, around thirty transit vans brimming with police were arriving. June 18, 1984 may well be remembered for many years to come in the industrial history of Britain. It was certainly the worst scenes of violence I had witnessed on the streets of Britain. There were repeated charges by horses and officers on foot with batons being used to quell the lines of pickets that were trying to reach the gates of the coke works.

Groups of riot squads were in amongst them trying to divide their numbers in to manageable groups that could be controlled by back-up squads of arresting officers. The policy was to divide and scatter so as to gain complete control of the road that led to the coke plant and even though many of the strikers crossed over a railway line to try and enter from the rear, they found themselves confronting more lines of police who had been guided from the observation helicopter. Some individuals did manage to break through the lines to try and draw the main body of police away from the gates by hurling masonry stripped from a boundary wall just before the arrival of the lorry convoy, but it was a futile attempt ending in most being arrested. There had been many injuries on both sides, including Mr Scargill who was quickly taken to Rotherham Hospital. It was estimated that at the height of the riot there had been around 8000 pickets in the area, but the end result was the convoy of lorries arrived, took on their loads and departed as they had done every day of the Orgreave conflict.

Although no one realised at the time, the miners cause was lost after this day. True it was to last for another eight months and there would be more violence at a number of pits, but nothing on the scale we had seen over the last four months. Nobody was claiming any glory amongst the crews we just did what we were briefed to do because, in simple language, that was our job. True we did feel loyalty for the company that was employing us and if we could produce something better than the opposition, then that was just old fashioned competition. ITN had played a major role in bringing the daily images to the screen with a total commitment to coverage on the ground. At the height of the trouble in South

Yorkshire, they had thirty two rooms booked at the Grosvenor Hotel in Sheffield.

Now the action moved to power stations, railway yards, haulage companies and even to river wharfs where foreign coal was being shipped in. The NUM were blaming the media for showing the downside of their conflict and yet looking back into my work diaries, I see we covered stories of family hardship, food distribution centres for miners, two children's pantomimes, a carol service and the sad story that miners were having to hand pets over to the RSPCA due to being unable to feed them. There were constant rumours that secret talks were being held between the NUM and the Coal Board and there was much press activity to try and discover the location. The Coal Board also wanted to show the conditions underground due to lack of maintenance during the strike and were also suggesting that some pits, although not earmarked for closure, may have to be abandoned. One of them was at Brodsworth, near Doncaster.

We arrived around eight p.m. and were preparing to go down to the bottom of the shaft which, according to Coal Board officials, would show the full extent of damage that had occurred over the last eight months caused by natural earth movement. Somehow news of our visit had reached the local pickets and very soon the whole pit area and yard was full of miners, determined to stop us going underground.

One of the pickets had been interviewed by the BBC and had declared that if the ITN film crew went down Brodsworth Pit, then they would make sure they did not come out. This was of course very distressing for our families who were aware of the area we were covering. By now the Coal Board officials were becoming concerned and had contacted the police for assistance as we were now confined to one room for safety. Even with police protection getting out was not going to be easy as we needed to reach the camera car. The alternative was to go out in a police van and leave the car unattended for at least twenty-four hours with the likelihood of it being trashed. The police arrived in force with around 500 officers and declared the mass picket on Coal Board property was illegal and threatened to arrest union officials unless they withdrew to the public road. At least this had the effect of clearing the immediate area and we were able to reach the car. Our instructions were to take up a place in the convoy of vans that was leaving, headed by a police car that would have sirens sounding and blue lights flashing in an attempt to distract those pickets nearest the road who may be thinking of hurling objects. We were fourth in line with two Transit vans front and rear and had been warned to keep out of sight, leaving Frank to do the high speed driving. As we sped past the main bunch, a house brick passed over the bonnet and struck the van in front and someone emptied the contents of a pint of beer over our windscreen making Frank comment about such a waste, but we made it to safety and after expressing our gratitude to the police chief headed for the safety of the Dragonara Hotel, Leeds.

We were on the road again at five a.m. heading towards the Selby Coalfield, the newest of Britain's pits. This was our first visit to the area and as we arrived the crowd showed their contempt for the press by letting off a volley of stones towards us. As I looked up the sky appeared to be full of black objects, not unlike a swarm of starlings, which were falling on us. The only defence was to turn and duck down to reduce the impact, nevertheless, we all took hits to parts of our body but fortunately not around the head. We cheered up by telling ourselves tomorrow was Saturday and we had been promised a 'stand down' day. As for me, I had a new VW Polo on order to be delivered at the weekend.

Monday morning was another five a.m. start to make another attempt to go down Brodsworth Pit. Once again the Coal Board were anxious to show the worsening conditions but we still had to pass the picket line who would now be aware of the purpose of our visit. It was almost like a bush telegraph system for within no more than ten minutes groups of miners were gathering at the entrance gate. Within the hour the police estimated there was a thousand. Once again the threat was made that if a film crew descended into the mine then they would make sure that they would not be able to get back up. The situation was now taking on a more serious side. Mines Safety Officers were concerned about the welfare of non accredited people entering the mine. The Legal department at ITN were making noises about possible claims and most of all the police were not happy about the possibility of a full scale riot about three people who had no immediate connection to the striking miners or the Coal Board. The matter was not our choice anymore. Frank and I were perfectly willing to go down the mine but it was the police who made the final decision after speaking to the ITN Newsdesk, the Coal Board and NUM officials. This was one battle the miners had won.

The next day found us at Silverwood Pit near Rotherham, yet another we had previously visited in the early hours of a nightly patrol. This was probably the last of any serious rioting the police had to deal with, this time the problem was burning barricades which had been erected at both sides of the pit entrance effectively blocking the whole approach road and preventing any charges by the mounted police, which was the object of the strikers. One police chief summed up the scene with what was probably the most plausible reason for the action when he said, "This is their final Trump on Judgement Day." I thought he was being a bit over melodramatic as he continued, "We're sick and tired of it and I expect you chaps are too. Nobody bothers to watch the news anymore." While I couldn't agree with all his opinions, he was right about the news bulletins no longer being compulsive viewing. This day at Silverdale was to mark the end of violent hostility and an end to mass picketing, scenes of which had been transmitted around the world, often being seen in overseas countries before it was shown in Britain. Now in their specially adapted vehicles, the police moved in and tossed aside the barriers and obstacles that had been built to deny them entry.

While it was happening, most miners stood and watched, their only resistance now reduced to chants of, "Facists", "Tory lackies", "Gestapo", and a string of left wing phrases from some who may not have been genuine miners. As for the ITN crews, we were growing weary of the same routine day after day. My work diary shows that from this day through to the return to work at the symbolic Cortonwood Pit on March 5, 1985, we only covered thirty stories connected to the miners' strike and some of these were to show miners returning to work and coal being produced again. Again there were rumours of secret talks between the NUM and the Coal Board, or as the National Press preferred to say, between Scargill and MacGregor. Frank and I had been given a change of story at the beginning of September to cover a murder trial that had grabbed the headlines due to its gruesome background. This resulted in the trial being moved to Durham and we booked in at a hotel only 200 metres from the Crown Court.

It was the usual routine with pictures of witnesses and legal teams arriving then waiting around until the lunchtime news should there have been any developments. The same applied for the early evening and late evening news. Once the Court had convened at ten a.m. we were free for at least two hours and with the hotel so convenient, it was the ideal place for morning coffee in the lounge and relax with the papers. Which is what we were doing on the second day when into the hotel lobby walked Arthur Scargill and his team of negotiators. The whole of the Fleet Street press and television newsdesks were scouring the country to find where the secret talks were being held and here we were with the answer in front of us. Mr Scargill was surprised when he saw us, asking what we were doing here. I beat a hasty retreat to the Court House and was let into the Press Gallery to catch our reporter's eye and tell her the news, which brought forth a rather unladylike response! Over at the hotel, Arthur was not going to divulge any information about the location of the talks, or even if any progress had been made, despite much friendly persuasion so what could have been the biggest story of the week faded when he and his team turned and left to find somewhere else for lunch. Not before one of his minders blocked the exit from the car park for several minutes to ensure they were not followed.

There were several more weeks of the cat and mouse game of 'find the settlement talks' until both sides finally announced that an agreement was close, but both were being 'tight lipped' about any details. The Coal Board were sticking to their plans for closing those pits that were unprofitable and geologically unsound, of which Cortonwood was high on the list. For the NUM they were insisting that when a return to work had finally been agreed, all the strikers at Cortonwood had to be reinstated and allowed to march back to work at their pit. While this may have appeared very emblematic, and of course we filmed it, had those same miners been able to see twenty years into the future, the 'fight to the end' which all of them claimed they would do, would have shown a very different scene. Now the site is a huge retail park drawing crowds from a large area and helping to keep the cash tills ringing are many miners and their families!

All of this had yet to happen and it was not until March 3, 1985 at the TUC Headquarters in London that the decision was taken to call off the strike with a full return to work on March 5. This was certainly welcomed by all the film crews, including ITN and as we were all based at the Grosvenor Hotel in Sheffield, an 'end of strike party' was planned in the coffee shop which the staff very kindly allowed us to take over, even making a cake suitably decorated with the ITN logo in addition to a seemingly endless supply of sandwiches and nibbles. It is difficult to describe the feeling of relief that we all felt after twelve months of torment, abuse, physical and mental fatigue and exasperation. The London crews had been worked turn and turn about, whereas Frank and I, along with Rick Richards and Ken Tebbenham, who were the local Yorkshire TV crew, had taken the brunt of the action by being in the area and on call. When we finally checked out of the hotel, we had spent nine weeks there and our only complaint was that in all that time, the menu never changed. But then how many normal guests stay for that length of time?

The coffee shop girls had worked wonders for us as we all sat down around seven p.m. to enjoy an evening of total relaxation. We totalled over twenty made up from six crews, plus reporters and editors and at first the atmosphere was convivial, that is until the mischievousness in all of us began to take over. Someone threw a peanut, somebody else retaliated. More peanuts were thrown and this time in return came bread buns. Then someone went behind the counter and returned with a tray of eggs (it could only have been Frank). Then the fun began, but not before someone brought out a roll of bin liners to protect our jackets after which it became a 'free for all'. This was our safety valve that was finally giving way to all the pent up tension that the last twelve months had served up. One of the girls at the reception desk later told me a story about a middle aged couple who checked in for an overnight stay, and having endured a long drive, wanted to relax over a pot of tea before retiring. As they made their way to the coffee shop door, an egg hit the inside of the glass panel and slowly slid down in front of them in the style of a slapstick comedy routine. They both stopped, looked at each other and without saying a word made their way to the lift. It was all over. Tomorrow we would be filming the return to work. First at a pit near Barnsley with 'King Arthur' leading his men, then at Cortonwood where it had all started just a year ago. As the miners proudly marched into their pit, one old retired miner was heard to comment, "Lions led by Donkeys."

For many months after this day, wherever film crews gathered to reminisce about the period and recall other stories from that age, it became common to enquire if they were speaking 'BM' or 'AM', or in other words, did they mean, 'before miners', or 'after miners'.

The spring like weather was continuing and one of the first nice 'picture' stories we covered in 'soft' news terms was the re-opening of the Blisworth canal tunnel in Northants after a four year closure for repairs. Our reporter was Jeremy Hands who we had spent many hours with on the nightly 'pit patrols'. He had covered many major news stories, including Middle East offensives and coverage of the Falklands War. Sadly, his life was tragically cut short at the age of forty seven by a mystery illness which it was believed he contracted abroad.

Our next 'headline' story that was to lead all bulletins for several days was the Bradford football ground fire tragedy. The actual fire was captured by live cameras, who, by coincidence were there to cover the match. When we arrived to interview survivors, it became a very moving experience listening to their stories of adversity, more so where they had lost a relative or friend and were finding difficulty in expressing their loss. I have often observed that in such circumstances, people feel it to be a way of coping with grief just to be able to relate to someone who can impart sympathy. Once again, as was so often the case, when we finally left Bradford it was to travel down to spend a day at Alton Towers and a new leisure park that was opening near Nottingham, where for the opening by boxer, Henry Cooper, they were to have a fly-past by Concorde. Such extremes of stories would be difficult to invent.

We did have a brief return to Sheffield for the start of the NUM Conference and even this was tinged with aggravation when the delegates from Nottinghamshire walked out. They had already proposed a breakaway union known as the Union of Democratic Mineworkers (UDM) and were proposing to take over the existing headquarters near Nottingham. This was a story that would run on for several weeks. Channel 4 News (which was supplied by ITN) did a number of in-depth stories on the legal background of a breakaway union, but as time has shown, it was a very well organised and efficient Union.

We also had two more visits to Bradford for the opening of the inquests on the victims of the fire, but once again, this was balanced with a trip to Hull to interview John Cleese, who was on location with the film 'Clockwise'. I had worked with John before in Birmingham, and although the object of the interview was the somewhat sombre topic of human rights, wherever John was it was difficult to be serious. He soon had reporter, Jane Corbin, in fits of laughter when, with a straight face he pointed to me and said, "You know all sound recordists are deaf don't you?"

Another disaster in 1985 occurred at Manchester Airport when a Boeing 737 belonging to British Airtours had an engine explode and the pilot had to abort the take off just before the end of the runway as he was approaching maximum speed. Fifty four passengers died in the smoke and flames that engulfed the rear of the fuselage. One more passenger died in hospital a week later. We were called around eight a.m. and despite heavy rush hour traffic, we were on location at ten a.m. It was to be a long day and one that marked the end of another stint with Frank. I felt it was time to take another sabbatical and devote yet more time to my minuscule record company. The Compact Disc was gaining a foothold with the record buying public and I could see that it had potential for the small producer. I would of course still be available for location work, but without the strain of round the clock availability.

With the introduction of the video camera and recorder, there had been a steadily growing market for corporate productions. Without the restrictions of film processing laboratories, more and more small companies were being established to enter into the field of industrial documentaries in the form of training films, advertising and publicity productions.

There were a number of corporate video companies formed in the Midlands so I was able to make myself available with or without sound equipment. Another change was the company who had taken over the ITV franchise for the Midlands. This was now known as Central Television and was operating from the same premises with all the old personnel and of course the eight floors of BBC Pebble Mill still dominated the Edgbaston skyline. It was now very much back to being a 'jobbing' recordist with jobs of no particular significance except to those who might be affected by the proposed route of the M40 motorway or the reopening of Snow Hill Station, Birmingham or even Sarah Ferguson visiting Cadbury's chocolate factory at Bourneville.

*

I also kept in touch with Frank and was available whenever Russ, who had taken my place, wanted a weekend off, or went off on a package holiday. There had been changes at ITN too. Cost cutting was now the order of the day and a number of staff cameramen and recordists had been offered early retirement (very early in some cases) and some were now out in the freelance market. Shaun Gilmartin was one who moved from London to the peace and tranquillity of Derbyshire and formed his own corporate company which made another work contact. I seemed to be still using the old system that Les and I had started way back in the sixties, where the principle of ten contacts offering ten days a year each would constitute a basic living. The fact that I have not complained about lunchtimes or lunches for a good number of pages indicates that it was still a sound formula (pun intended).

One major disaster that I missed during my 'resting' spell was that at Hillsborough, Sheffield. However, exactly twelve months later while working with Shaun, we covered the start of the inquest along with interviews with survivors and yet another background piece. 1991 marked a milestone for a story I had first covered with Frank back in 1974. This was the start of the appeal at the Old Bailey by the six prisoners accused of the Birmingham bombs. It was the culmination of a long campaign by a number of groups who had questioned the original evidence on which the six had been convicted. It was very much a waiting game and any hopes of an announcement during the first week were soon dashed. The press corps had already spent a week penned in a specially built compound with TV cameras at the front and the 'stills boys' at the rear on step ladders. The only saving grace was the abundance of takeaway sandwich and coffee shops. When Friday came all we could do was head for Euston Station and do it all over again the next week. Not one of us complained about letting the train take the strain.

We started out again on the Sunday evening for Euston and for once, the West Coast Main Line was free of weekend engineering works which meant an almost on time arrival and an early night ready for the Monday morning fray. This meant being at the 'press pen' by seven a.m. to ensure we had a front row spot. Monday and Tuesday turned into long days of just waiting for news, broken only by an interview with one of the original campaigners for their release, to which reporter, Mark Foster, added a 'piece to camera' and the package went down the line for BBC Midlands Today. Wednesday brought a flurry of excitement from the Court. A statement was expected to be issued and in preparation, BBC Radio placed microphones with multi connections for access by all media channels. But again, by five p.m. word came out that last minute legal disputes would mean an overnight adjournment. It was all going to happen tomorrow, Thursday. My cameraman from the start had been Geoff Ward, but as he had a prior engagement on Thursday at a church in the West Midlands, a replacement was being sent down. I was always apprehensive over crew changes during long location shoots. Just like any other job, patterns of understanding and work methods that one team put together always mean the final result is so much smoother and unruffled.

Any concern I may have had about the change of cameraman disappeared when into the hotel walked Paul Hunt, from Nottingham. Paul had come up the old fashioned way as a film cameraman and was no slouch when it came to using a stills camera either. Like so many other technicians, he had taken the changeover to video in his stride and we had already done many stories together. What ever happened tomorrow was going to be a memorable moment which meant an early night and as Paul's drive down into Central London had been unpleasant, he didn't argue with that.

The 'press pen' was becoming a social gathering of photographers, reporters and crews each day. The numbers had swelled as the final outcome of the hearing neared and there was a great deal of interest from overseas, to say nothing of that in the whole of Ireland. A number of ITN staff men who had served their time on the miners' strike, came up to ask about how Frank and I were coping with life 'AM'. (After Miners for those who may have skipped earlier pages). One of them related the story of the final party in the coffee shop in Sheffield and confessed to me that he had always been worried about who cleaned up the mess. I was able to finally reassure him that a very generous collection was taken for the girls to ease their burden.

The time for the six to walk out of the Old Bailey had now been fixed for four p.m. and all the usual line up preparation for picture and sound were being made. It was then we were told that we would be interrupting racing from the Cheltenham Festival to bring live pictures that would be transmitted around the world. For my part, the thought of yet another possible epitaph one liner came to mind, but for Paul he was concerned that this was certainly the biggest live inject story he had worked on and should there be a camera problem, it would be a mark against him for the rest of his career. Someone had told me early in my career that there was no substitute for experience and it was now to show through. Paul was a very capable cameraman, even serving his time on the miners' strike, but he was twenty years my junior. All I did to bolster his confidence was put a hand on his shoulder and tell him that it was just another live inject. No different from many others we had done in the East Midlands into the evening news.

We had with us as reporter, Joshua Rozenberg, who was the BBC's legal correspondent and to help Paul's confidence, I whispered to him that now would be a good time to get some free legal advice about buying a house. Then it all happened. With a nod from the floor manager we were live into the network as the six lined up in front of the static microphones while several dozen camera shutters clicked incessantly. Joshua moved into position while I did a quick check with Paul to ensure the short gun microphone was out of frame and we were 'on air'. Joshua's piece was faultless and when finished Paul panned the camera onto the reactions of the six released men leaving me to record the atmosphere. Then it was all over, well almost. Someone had mentioned to a radio reporter that I had been there on the night of the Birmingham bombing and he was asking if I had any opinion. Did I want to have my fifteen minutes of fame? I was remembering what the late Eamonn Andrews had said once during an interview when asked about opinions, which was, "We don't have them. We cannot take sides." The next day we drove down to a riverside hotel near Maidenhead where we were able to film three of the released men relaxing for the first time in almost seventeen years as free men. As I had driven out of London, I offered to drive the remainder of the journey back to the Midlands, going via Coventry to leave Mark at the station. It was only a short trip to my home from there and as we parted, Paul took my hand and said, "Thanks for yesterday." His real reward came in the 'herogram' we both received from the London Newsdesk.

As I walked in the door the phone was ringing. It was a call from a Birmingham cameraman asking if I was free tomorrow, Saturday. As it was only a few miles away to interview Terry Venables, then the Manager of Tottenham Hotspur, I said yes despite the pile of mail waiting to be opened. CDs and cassettes were still selling in sufficient quantities, enough that is to keep the accountant agreeing that there was still a profit margin. What was more noticeable were the working days now committed to film and TV income. These were certainly reducing when compared to the 1980s but then this was my choice to some extent. I was beginning to see myself as something of a veteran when I looked around at my associates and this was more or less confirmed while I was doing a local story on training football apprentices. The trainer was using a public address system to instruct the players where to stand and one such instruction went along the lines of, "Move down the right wing to where that grey haired soundman is standing." My first reaction was to look and see who he was referring to, until I realised it was me!

An Election was called for April, 1992 and I was booked for a four-week contract attached to BBC East Midlands in Nottingham. The cameraman was to be Dave Webb who I had known from the time when he worked as the lighting man with Frank for ITN. He had first made the move over to sound, then like many other recordists, he graduated to the camera department. Dave already had a contract with East Midlands, so it meant the work would not be nationwide.

Based on previous election campaigns I had covered, the routine would be to follow the 'big guns' as they toured the hustings and the first week brought out, David Plunkett, Norman Lamont, Kenneth Baker and Roy Hattersley. Local MPs Kenneth Clarke and Margaret Beckett were being featured almost daily as they toured in support of some of the more rural areas. April 9 was Polling Day and we took our places at Derby to follow the count after the Polling stations closed. The two big names here were Edwina Currie and Margaret Beckett and by five a.m. it was becoming clear that it was going to be a Tory victory.

Towards the end of the year, Birmingham was chosen to host a European Summit which meant there was a need for crews to cover all the foreign TV companies who had sent reporters over. It was a way to broaden one's horizons and learn a new language at the same time. Dave Webb and I covered reports for Anntena TV Greece, TV1 Finland, NRK 1 Norway and ZDF Germany.

Horizons were to broaden again in 1993 when the World Badminton Championships were held at the new Indoor Arena in

Birmingham. This time the countries were SAT 1 from Germany, Iceland TV and Malayan TV. But a pleasant way to start the New Year was meeting up again with Brian Clough when he was given the Freedom of the City in Nottingham. "Where have you been young man?" was the first thing he said as we walked out onto the Town Hall balcony. Another first was a booking from Sky Sport to go down to Silverstone to interview F1 driver Mika Hakkinen who had just been appointed to the McLaren race team. As he came into the race garage the first thing he did was to come over and shake our hands and introduce himself.

As the year tailed off I did a quick tally of working days on TV productions and found it to be twenty less than the previous year even though Frank and I were back together for the last month. ITN had made further cutbacks by taking away the camera car and equipment. Now it was back to using our own transport on a mileage basis and having to use equipment that was not in the 'bloom of youth'. Was this the beginning of the end? 1994 was certainly going to be a year of changes.

CHAPTER FIVE

THE DINOSAUR YEARS

Why Dinosaur? My Chambers Twentieth Century Dictionary gives one definition of the word as a fossil or anything dating from an earlier age. I was now aware of the fact that at every location shoot I was the oldest person on the crew and while this would not normally be a problem, I was realising that there was an ever increasing gap in likes and dislikes, in food, in music, in films, in TV programmes, in dress style, in speech, in courtesy, manners and dignity and in worldly knowledge. Mentioning the war, National Service or even the 'swinging sixties' brought out the boredom in many. I had perhaps stayed in my job too long. Technology was now taking over. This was brought home to me when I was once asked by a news editor who must have been at least twenty two, if I could go and record some effects for a background programme he was working on. When I mentioned what I needed to obtain a quality recording, his reply was, "I don't want quality, I want it by lunchtime."

Like so many other business organisations, age was no longer associated with experience and in television with its myth of a glamorous life, it perhaps drew a type of person who may well have been creative but lacking in commitment. Cost was now uppermost in all productions with accountants to oversee every aspect of the output. The regional outposts of the BBC were those which suffered badly from cuts in programme making. Some of the regional documentaries I worked on for Pebble Mill in Birmingham often reminded me of the Empire Reel films I first started with back in the early sixties, when we were constantly reminded that there would be no lavish locations or luxury hotels.

It was going to be a year of 'last times', one of which occurred in April when, following the takeover of Rover Cars by BMW, I was booked for my last trip overseas to Munich and Regensburg by BBC Midlands. They wanted to see how the lives of German car workers compared with those who worked in the West Midland factories. All in all it was a pleasant trip, starting at Bavarian Television headquarters in Munich, where the Head of Programmes made us feel we were far more important than we thought. This welcome continued when we visited the car factories making the whole visit a most enjoyable one. It also enabled us to take in some of the sights and local culture which is rare when on location and a tight budget. It was the same crew I had worked with at the Old Bailey on the Birmingham Six story, Geoff Ward, camera and Mark Foster the reporter.

I had only been back in England three days when Frank rang me with some shattering news. ITN were now looking to change their regional policy for news coverage now that the 'Betacam' system had more or less been perfected. With this method of combined camera and recorder one man could, after a fashion, go out and cover news stories using the auto-record circuitry with a reporter holding the microphone. Quality was not a consideration. They wanted it by lunchtime! This meant that from the end of July, they were taking back the camera and recording equipment and cancelling any agreement for work allocation (it had, after all, only been a verbal agreement). Frank was sixty four, I was sixty.

The Midlands crew that had been formed in 1974 and had produced some of the biggest news stories during that period was to be disbanded, but not before going out on a 'high' with one last major story that was to run on all bulletins for eighteen days and capture the hearts of the nation during that time. This story was not one of disaster but a most harrowing tale of deception in one of the most audacious kidnap cases in British history. A new born baby girl was taken from the arms of her father only hours after being born and while the mother was only in the next room in the maternity unit at the Nottingham Queen's Medical Centre.

We were called to the Nottingham Hospital at seven p.m. on the first day of July with the brief that a baby named Abbie had been kidnapped. Not unnaturally, the parents were too distraught to give any details, but a police liaison team were on hand to hold a press conference and outline the background to the disappearance. A woman dressed as a nurse had entered the unit while the father was enjoying the first moments with his new daughter, she told him that the baby needed to have a routine hearing test and she would only be two rooms away down the corridor. Unwittingly, the father handed over the baby and when the mother returned a moment or so later and was told the story, she knew instinctively that something was wrong and by the time both ran into the corridor, there was no sign of the woman or the baby.

The police had very few clues to work on, except some grainy closed circuit television pictures of the woman leaving the maternity department and the main hospital entrance. As Frank said on our way back to the camera car, "This story could run and run." For the next two days there was little in the way of pictures for the Newsdesk. Seeing police carrying out house to house enquiries does have its limitations and even the police admitted they were struggling. For the start of the new week ITN sent up the satellite truck and mobile edit suite, expecting that there would be some good news to report very soon. There was still no access to the parents and all questions at the daily press conference were answered by the police teams. One small event that London thought to be very news worthy and certainly the police were anxious to show, if only to keep public awareness to the fore was the message of goodwill sent by Princess Diana to the parents.

Each day we were sending live reports for all bulletins as the 'media circus' grew and it was becoming a reunion of old faces from our past, but there was still no news of Abbie. The week dragged on through another weekend until on the Monday morning we had a six fifteen a.m. call to get to Nottingham police headquarters, where it was reported a man had information about a new baby that had suddenly appeared at a neighbour's house. This turned out to be a hoax call and was a cruel blow for the parents and did not even make a picture story for the first news of the day. At the police press conference it was reported that police had twice visited the house of a young woman who was on probation and had a long list of psychiatric troubles and who had been telling neighbours she was pregnant, but as yet they had nothing to hold her on.

Four more days went by with the same routine of a daily press conference, a live lunchtime news report and some library footage of police search teams. We were now into day fifteen. It was Saturday July 16 when my phone rang at four a.m. The baby had been found at the house where the police had already visited. The twenty-two-year-old woman had confessed to abducting the baby from the maternity ward at Nottingham Queen's Medical

Centre. At six a.m. we were doing a live piece into the early morning programmes, then a press conference with a jubilant police team. This was followed later in the day with a photo call at a nearby Hilton Hotel when the world were seeing pictures of the parents and of course, Abbie, who was sleeping through most of it and completely unaware of the drama she had been involved in. On the Sunday the police held their last gathering for the press where a whole range of photographs and evidence was made available taken inside the house where Abbie had been hidden.

As always on these occasions when the 'media circus' moves into town there are winners and losers. On this occasion it was a small baker's shop, also serving takeaway drinks, in the little suburb of Nottingham known as West Bridgford. Here we had become on first name terms with the girls behind the counter, to such an extent that by the final week we were using the backdoor to avoid queuing. But then, as always, the circus left town.

Monday, July 18, was to be our last day on the story. The girl responsible was to make her first court appearance and we covered this with live injects into the news at ten twenty a.m., twelve thirty p.m. and five forty p.m. If we were going out in glory, this was the way to do it by being the lead story on all bulletins. Then it was all over. People drifted away. There were no messages of goodwill, but then I don't suppose either of us expected any. We had seen the highs and lows over the last twenty years and had always held onto the old freelance adage that you are only as good as your last job.

For Frank, it really was the end of the road. He had never been freelance in the true sense of the word. His career began in 1957 with Birmingham Commercial Films, which at that time were supplying the film facilities for the then Midland ITV franchise holder, Alpha Television. ATV took over in 1960 and the staff formed the new film unit. In the mid sixties, he went out to Zambia to set up the new television network which was one of the first ambitions of the then new President, Kenneth Kaunda. Internal politics and cultural differences saw Frank back in Britain before the end of his original contract and, although back at ATV, he was now working in a lower grade. As mentioned in earlier pages, it was the offer of work from ITN due to his midland location that had originally brought us together.

He had never built up a network of contacts so all his work was limited to two main sources. As for me I was still using my old formula of ten contacts each giving me ten days' work in a year, although now I was tending to be more selective. The glory days were behind me. I was no longer interested in prestigious locations with named stars and convoluted plots and screen credits. At least the years had taught me that seeing my name on a cheque was a far better way to put a smile on the bank manager's face.

The remainder of the year fitted nicely around the weeks when I was wearing my record producer hat and was made up mainly of three regional documentaries produced at BBC Pebble Mill, Birmingham. However, there was one nice link to bygone days when I was booked to cover the launch of Brian Clough's autobiography which then led to a mini documentary entitled, 'Goodbye to Cloughie'. It was a sad occasion in one way because Brian's health had deteriorated and it showed in his face and speech. There was one nice touch though which I regret that the editor chose to leave out, when Brian was talking about being around too long, then he pointed to me, just standing out of shot and recording what he was saying, and said, "Even Ken knows what I mean."

The variety of jobs was now becoming very uninteresting almost to a state of 'just going through the motions'. I had to keep telling myself that this was regional television with very limited viewing figures, but somewhere out there it would be of interest. Even referring to my work diaries does not bring anything exciting to mind. Again there were three Pebble Mill documentaries, plus some coverage of celebrations of the fortieth anniversary of VE Day with traditional street parties. Perhaps the highlight was covering the testimonial for Gordon Banks, one of the greatest goalkeepers of the Twentieth Century. In his career he made 628 appearances for England and his famous save against Pele in the 1970 World Cup is still talked about as one of the greatest. On YouTube, it has had over three quarters of a million hits.

The workload for 1996 was now down to thirty-two days, partly by choice but also due to changing patterns in programme production. Technology was again being used where manpower costs could be saved and this was also evident in the nightly regional news programmes. There was, however, some variety when the BBC decided to take the local news out on the road and produce the whole programme from different towns around the Midlands. This at last brought back some of the former working ways, where the need of a sound recordist recording three channels of dialogue on location and live into the programme did have that feel of yesteryear.

Another job which turned into a minor reunion and one of the last times that I would work for Central Television was a programme about house renovation. This featured Paul Hunt on camera and, now turned to directing, Shaun Gilmartin my old colleague from ITN.

As I celebrated New Year's Day, 1997, little did I know that this was going to be my final year as a Sound Recordist. I was aware of the reduction of working days in television brought about by my own decision to expand my record company and possibly being aware that the day had to come when either myself, or perhaps someone else would tell me I was 'over the hill', although I hoped it would be couched in much more pleasant terms. There were three jobs in January, increasing to four in February. None of which were outstanding in terms of sound artistry. In March there were two stories for 'Newsround', the popular programme introduced by John Craven and intended to bring news to a young audience in a less sombre presentation than the late night bulletins.

1997 was also the year that brought a Labour Government, led by Tony Blair, back to Westminster. I had in fact turned down an offer of two weeks work covering the run up period to Polling Day due to working on two record releases. However, I can say that I featured in the aftermath of the Labour landslide when I was called to Derby on the day after the results to interview the MP who had soundly beaten Edwina Currie. With Tony Blair at 'Number Ten' it brought to an end one of my many mythical epitaphs which was, I had worked with every Prime Minister since Harold MacMillan, although I have to clarify that by saying they may not all have been in office at the time. David Cameron was of course years into the future.

One of many things that Mrs Thatcher changed was the legislation that allowed independent production companies to make programmes for the television networks which hitherto had been a closed door to any freelance producers. Writers were the only people who could introduce their own input for BBC and ITV productions and of course I am speaking of the period before the proliferation of satellite dishes, Freesat and Freeview. Now there was a mushrooming of small companies who were able to create mainstream programmes at a big saving in cost which was now the all important consideration.

Two of these independent companies provided me with some of my final location work. One was on a programme entitled 'Enthusiasts' which looked at some of the more extreme hobbies that people pursued, although I began to have my doubts that some would have no more than a following of one! The working title for the programme was 'Nutters' which may indicate some of the people we had to deal with and keep a straight face during each interview. Take the man who was dedicated to the flanged wheel! This was the type of wheel that railways all over the world had been using since the opening of the Stockton and Darlington Railway in 1825 and he spoke of it with such passion, one could be forgiven for thinking he was behind the idea. Prior to this, as he kept reminding the reporter, man was using the ordinary cart wheel with the flange on the rail and had he continued to do so, rail travel would have been much slower. He spoke at such a rapid pace about his enthusiasm, that we had to keep slowing him down, not only to understand what he was saying, but to allow the tape editors at a later stage to be able to use the material in the programme.

He had obviously made this a lifelong study and had researched many locations where the flanged wheel was being used, other than on railway vehicles. So we found ourselves at a cricket ground near Chesterfield, where the sight screen was on rails. Then to a church in the West Midlands where rows of pews were on rails to allow them to be moved according to the size of the congregation. At each location he went into raptures and had to be curtailed.

In the apple orchards of Worcestershire, we found a huge greenhouse that moved on rails and could be positioned to allow the workers to gather the crop in a fraction of the time it would take with restricted access. There was another more sedate location at a stately home out towards Oswestry where a sunhouse could be propelled on rails to follow the movement of the sun's rays. I think this was the location where he informed us that he was writing a reference work on the subject. We all smiled politely and wished him every success. As we loaded the vehicles, I recall the director saying, "It could only happen in England couldn't it."

Another 'enthusiast' we visited had a passion for battery powered transport and had modified everything from a bicycle to an arm chair. This was around the time when the Government were relaxing the taxation classes for non polluting vehicles so this must have been his driving force for he had, literally, turned an ordinary upholstered arm chair into a road going vehicle, complete with number plates, indicators, front and rear lights, horn and a seat belt. The steering was by some means of tiller method which connected to the wheels which ran on axles. The original castors having been dispensed with. What we were not aware of was that the number plates had originally been fitted to a scooter and had no legal standing on this contraption. That was the word used by the police officer who was to appear later. It seems we were all guilty of aiding and abetting when we asked if we could film him driving around the village, to which he was only too keen to oblige, pointing out that he had applied for a

Patent on his method of steering and did not want any close up views of this. Perhaps he had a vision of some wealthy benefactor taking up the idea and making him a rich man. So off he ventured down the village main street and after a complicated turn, was back with us eager for another attempt. So was our director, who suggested that this time we follow in the camera car. When he had been describing the specification of the, I must use the word contraption again, no one recalled him mentioning brakes and this was his undoing, and ours. An elderly lady had parked outside the village shop, an exercise she probably performed every day. She may well have looked in her rear view mirror for an approaching car before opening her driving door, possibly having dismissed a moving arm chair as not a road hazard.

She opened her door just as the arm chair was alongside, catching the arm and forcing the door to open further, to the limit of the hinges in fact. Our intrepid inventor was jolted round, the chair performing two or three pirouettes before coming to rest on the grass. Just who rang the police we were never aware. The chances of a Panda car appearing in a country village in the middle of the afternoon were too much to put this down to coincidence.

As the officer was getting out, Gerry the cameraman was already saying, "It's nothing to do with us Guv!" I was about to join in the mock innocence when I shouted that the arm chair was on the move, which it was, as the inventor was making a getaway towards a recreation area. That spurred the constable into action on what up to now may have been a slow day for him, but his pursuit by car was thwarted by concrete posts across the entrance, which had not interrupted the chair's progress. We were right behind as he jumped out and proceeded to follow on foot recreating a scene that must have been straight out of 'The Goodies' or even 'Python'.

He made good progress and apprehended the 'chair' when the owner realised there was no way out. We were on the scene too, but any conversation that passed between them was lost, as the constable insisted that we were not to film or record the 'arrest'.

I always felt that Gerry was a little too honest in not running the camera from an innocent looking hand held position, I could clearly hear everything on the gun microphone.

I did mention this to him when we had made statements but he felt he had done the diplomatic thing. The director, Simon, who was also a partner in the production company, agreed with him on the grounds that there may be legal problems to follow. There was indeed a legal problem. The little old lady had forgotten to renew her road fund licence, thereby making any insurance claim null and void. What happened to the inventor? I never found out if the police took any action against him. He obviously did not find his rich benefactor as you don't see many powered arm chairs around our roads!

The last programme I worked on for an independent production company had a very interesting theme. This was for a programme called 'Witness' and gave an interesting and even worrying insight into how people recalled events they had seen to a court of law. Whenever I read of evidence in a trial being the main reason for conviction, my thoughts always return to this programme and some of the amazing events that made people give the verdict they believed in.

It was filmed in front of an audience of around one hundred ordinary citizens and all participants were chosen from them to represent a jury in a court room. The first example of how reliable a witness may be was given with a test of elapsed time. The audience was asked to indicate how much time had passed and to help with no distractions, all the main lights in the hall were dimmed, then a bell was sounded for the start and they had to raise a hand when they thought one minute had passed. Unbelievably, one lady raised an arm after eight seconds. In case anyone should think that this may be a weakness in the feminine psyche, the next two hands belonged to young gentlemen who thought they were accurate at sixteen and nineteen seconds.

The next test was based on the children's party game of Chinese Whispers and twelve people were selected from the audience, six men and six women as it might be on a jury. The first was given a story taken from an actual police report which read as follows, 'Four men stopped outside the Post Office in a blue car. Two of them went inside, while the other two went round the back of the premises. Two more vehicles drew up, one being a builder's truck the other being driven by a disabled driver, who asked the driver of the truck if he would be so kind as to post a letter for him as getting in and out of the car was difficult. Just then one of the men returned from the rear of the Post Office and snatched the letter from the disabled driver and ran off. The driver of the truck chased after him and while he was absent the second man came from the rear of the premises and drove off in the builder's truck. The alarm began to sound in the Post Office and two men dashed out carrying a red Post Office delivery sack and jumped into the blue car just as a police car arrived to intercept them. They both tried to evade arrest and got in with the disabled driver who made an attempt to start his car but due to the battery being flat he was unable to start the engine.

Sergeants Baker and Green arrested them, while two constables, Blake and Patterson chased after the man who had stolen the letter and with the help of the truck driver, apprehended him.

Those familiar with the party game will know that this message is passed on to the second, third, fourth and so on, until the story unfolds at the final person and a comparison is made with the original story.

What came out was along the lines of, "Four men tried to rob a Post Office in a green car but as this would not start they tried to escape in a builder's truck, knocking over an invalid who was trying to post a letter. They then ran off chased by two police constables who arrested them at the rear of the Post Office."

By now a number of people in the audience were beginning to wonder about the accuracy of statements as presented in evidence. Even our director passed the remark that, "After hearing that, it makes you wonder about history!" But there was more to come and for this, a company had been brought in to assemble a screen and film projector to show some motoring films taken in a typical English small town. This test was meant to obtain peoples' impression of the speed of a vehicle when driving through built up areas and whether they thought the speed limit was being broken.

Cards were handed round for comments to a series of questions that would be asked after each film, the first of which depicted a car with a noisy exhaust passing down a narrow street, the question being, was the car exceeding the 30 mph speed limit? Then the same car was seen passing along a wide dual carriageway with again the question of excessive speed above the limit. The scene now changed to a small saloon car driving along the same routes of narrow and wide roads and, again the same questions were asked about exceeding the speed limit. The answers were remarkable. Virtually everyone said the car with the noisy exhaust system was travelling at more than 30 mph in the narrow street, when in fact it was under the limit. When it was shown on the dual carriageway, most people said it was travelling at 30 mph, when in actual fact it was five miles an hour over.

With regard to the small saloon, the audience listed that in each case it was not breaking the speed limit, when in reality, it was breaking the law by five miles an hour. This was rather disturbing for it showed that people took the noise into consideration as part of their judgement, also a narrow street gave a greater impression of speed than a wide highway.

The final test of witness accuracy and certainly one that left everyone with some doubt in their minds had to be set up with a little deception. Once again twelve people were chosen and they were told that they had to listen to and count the number of chimes from a striking clock. However, for this sequence, eleven of them had been told to answer eleven when in fact the clock struck only ten times. The end result was uncanny to say the least.

Each witness was wearing headphones so they were unable to indicate to the next person how many they had counted. Also the audience were unable to hear the chimes, so preventing any possibility of the number being shown. When it came to the end and each witness was asked for the total, they began answering eleven as previously arranged until it came to the twelfth man. I, and I'm sure the rest of the crew expected him to say something along the lines of, "Well actually I made it ten." Or perhaps, "I may have miscounted but I thought it was ten." With all attention now on him, from the compére, who was also the director, the audience, the film crew and all the lights and microphones, his answer was 'eleven'. It was an astonishing example of someone going along with the majority and not wanting to appear foolish in front of others. I found it to be a salient lesson in the ways of my fellow man.

We were now into the high summer of 1997 and by coincidence, the last two stories of my career were connected with the weather. For some time past the BBC had been featuring the girls who read the weather forecasts in small location stories and it had proved to be such a success with viewers that they began to call it the 'Weather Show'. June was proving to be one of the wettest on record so it was going to be a damp ending to my life and times as a sound recordist. It all ended in the middle of a field in Leicestershire! The young girl had come totally unprepared for muddy fields so was in for a shock when the director told her the opening shot was her walking across the field to meet a scarecrow.

By luck, I had a spare pair of wellington boots but the size ten were not very flattering for her dainty feet, with the result that every step she took as the mud got deeper, the boot would come off and she would be ankle deep in the mire. By the time the scarecrow was reached, the tears were rolling down her cheeks and she was probably wishing she was somewhere else. I had fitted a radio microphone to her and as we were all still at the edge of the field, I was the only one who could hear her suffering as it started to rain. The rest of the crew were laughing about some previous night's programme on TV and as they were all under the age of thirty, I presumed it was probably Red Dwarf or The Young Ones, neither of which I found funny. With the thought of this, the falling rain and the sound of the girl whimpering in my headphones, a monumental decision was taken in the middle of this Leicestershire field. I really did not need this and I had reached the end of my career. At least it was me who was saying I was 'over the hill' and it was time to quit before becoming a complete fossil.

With the decision made there were no voices from the past, no flashbacks, no recalling past events. I had the rest of my life to do that, which I am able to do now as I muse about some of the things I have heard during recordings, such as answers to reporter's questions. I recall an occasion in Southampton when the Council were giving some consideration to legalising their 'Red Light District'. The reporter's question to one of the 'girls' was what did she think of the idea, to which the answer was, "I don't think the girls will stand for it."

In a slightly similar vein of humour, one well known lady Cabinet Minister was asked what it was like to be working amongst all the men replied, "For the first time in my life all the men are under me."

Then there was the man from the Treasury who said, "The deficit is due to the outgoing Government who only plastered over the cracks. We intend to do the job properly and paper over them."

Or the shamed MP who said, "I have no secrets between my wife. If she has any it's her private affair."

Or the recently elected MP who said, "I intend to push through this Bill on litter and all those who write me protest letters I shall tear them up and throw them to the four winds."

And perhaps one more before leaving the zany world of politics, there was the Tory MP who delivered, "Why do these workers and protesters have to leave such a mess after the strike, don't they realise that the ballot box is provided for their convenience."

Did someone once say that we only get the politicians we deserve? One final character that I spent many hours with on location was a director named Henry who, although very much at ease with all the modern things of life around him, was set in the past. He had in fact worked at Lime Grove Studios in London prior to the Second World War and was now just seeing out his days on documentaries and small feature productions. Nobody was really sure if it was his dry droll wit or whether he had some sort of verbal dyslexia when it came to using words, but invariably they were always wrong.

We were once covering a Catholic celebration when a breathless newspaper photographer came up and asked if he was too late and had he missed the service. Henry merely told him he had plenty of time as they were holding a Rectum Mass. The photographer looked at all our blank faces, wondering which one was going to laugh first, then when nobody did just turned round and left. All Henry said was, "He's a bit of an odd cove."

On another occasion, also within a church, we had been discussing religion on a fairly general level with the Bishop of Hereford, when Henry came out with, " It's those people with stones that commit the first sin, by the way, how many tunes will the choir be singing?"

I sometimes wondered if he had some mental block about religion, for another of his 'gaffes' was when he told someone that, "You need the patience of Solome and the wisdom of Joe to do my job."

Another occasion as we were packing up to leave, Henry got into his car and said, "Go forth and multiply yourselves." If I had to choose a favourite 'Henryism', it could only be the one he came out with when we were filming Simon Rattle when he had been appointed Assistant Conductor of the Bournemouth Symphony Orchestra.

The subject had got around to tenors who were prominent in 1974 and when the conversation lapsed, Henry added, "Yes they are all right but not a patch on Eric Crusoe."

There was a time when I toyed with the idea of publishing a list of his 'Spoonlexisms' as I intended calling them. The title I had in mind was, 'Citizens of the world, you're right'. And finally, in the best ITN tradition, there is always the British public who, as any comedian will tell you, are the best source for humour. We were once doing some 'vox pops' on New Year's Day, when the reporter asked a couple if they kept a diary. "No, said the lady, "we get our milk at the supermarket."

In this age of high speed technology, I can only marvel at today's equipment and what it can achieve, although I doubt if I am the only one from my generation that can sometimes see the join where quality has been relaxed in order to meet that 'lunchtime' deadline. A quality that would not have been transmitted fifty years ago. And yet I smile when I hear many old terms still in use by young reporters and newscasters. Such phrases as, we are sending a film crew. Or, we are bringing you footage live from the scene. Or, we are only able to show a few frames. All of these are leftovers from the days of film.

I am taking great care not to make the fatal mistake of using such words or clichés as final reel, or fade out, or final curtain as I come to the end of my story. It had started in 1954 during service with the RAF when a film unit came on the camp and as is the way in military affairs, anyone with a loosely connected interest in the cinema is assigned to the job. The same applies to musicians when a piano needs moving! I was given the job of showing them where the various locations were and I became so fascinated by the job of the sound recordist it made me want to follow the profession.

After all these years I still have that same spirit and enthusiasm as that first day when I walked along Rodmarton Street in London. It became my chosen life, hard at times, disappointing and frustrating as well and though I may now be much wiser, on the whole I enjoyed it.